PROBLEMS IN UNDERSTANDING RELIGIOUS RADICALIZATION IN SOUTH ASIA

The Regional Centre for Strategic Studies (RCSS) is a South Asian regional think tank, based in Colombo, Sri Lanka. Established in 1993, it is an independent, non-profit and non-governmental organization which encourages research, dialogue, and deliberation on a broad range of conventional and non-conventional sources of conflict. The RCSS enables scholars and other professionals to address, individually and collectively, problems and issues of topical interest for all South Asian countries.

The Centre's key objectives are to:

- Sponsor, coordinate, and support research on South Asian strategic, security, and environmental issues.
- Promote interaction among scholars and professionals in the region and beyond who are engaged in South Asian studies.
- Foster linkages and collaboration among institutions focusing on studies and activities related to conflict, conflict transformation, and regional cooperation in South Asia.
- Encourage a new generation of analysts and commentators to generate fresh ideas and perspectives on the security discourse in the region.

This publication was made possible by the Kodikara Award for South Asian Strategic Studies.

Contact address:
Regional Centre for Strategic Studies
68/1, Sarasavi Lane
Colombo-08
Sri Lanka
Tel: + (94) 11-2690913, 2690914
Fax: + (94) 11-2690769
E-mail: info@rcss.org
Website: www.rcss.org

RCSS Policy Studies 54

Problems in Understanding Religious Radicalization in South Asia

Perspectives on Islam and Hinduism

SHAHAB ENAM KHAN

REGIONAL CENTRE FOR STRATEGIC STUDIES
COLOMBO

MANOHAR
2013

Published by
Ajay Kumar Jain *for*
Manohar Publishers & Distributors
4753/23 Ansari Road, Daryaganj
New Delhi 110 002
and
Regional Centre for Strategic Studies
68/1, Sarasavi Lane
Colombo-08
SRI LANKA
Tel: + (94) 11-2690913, 2690914; Fax: + (94) 11-2690769
E-mail: info@rcss.org
Website: www.rcss.org

First published 2013

ISBN 978-93-5098-004-0

Printed at
Salasar Imaging Systems
Delhi 110 035

Contents

Acknowledgements

I would like to extend my sincere appreciation and deepest gratitude to the Regional Centre for Strategic Studies, Colombo, for the financial support to conduct this research study.

It took me a long time to write this study on the endless subject of 'radicalization', though not as long as it takes to write a doctoral thesis on quantum physics, surprisingly! I would like to express my sincere thanks to my colleagues at Jahangirnagar University and at the Bangladesh Enterprise Institute (BEI), who relentlessly helped me during this time. In particular, my young associates Faria Sultana, Ezadus Salam and Samila Haque—they practically turned into radicals as their work suffered terribly due to my focus on radicalism instead of on their work!

I must thank Humayun Kabir, Senior Research Director at BEI, for his valuable inputs and clear, accurate comments, which helped me refine my arguments. I must thank Farooq Sobhan, President, Bangladesh Enterprise Institute, for his fiery dragon breath on the ignominious earlier drafts! I should also thank Moonis Ahmar, University of Karachi, Pakistan; Sanjay Bhardwaj, Jawaharlal Nehru University, India; and Abul Kalam Azad, Chair of the Department of International Relations, Jahangirnagar University, Bangladesh, for their invaluable comments in finalizing this paper.

Finally, and most importantly, I am very grateful to my wife, Eashita Farzana Haque. For many months, she tolerated my erratic moods, and did not complain when I sat in my chair for hours, staring into space instead of engaging in conversation; I have been a less-than-ideal husband this entire while!

Dhaka SHAHAB ENAM KHAN
21 February 2012

CHAPTER ONE

Introduction to the Idea of Religious Radicalization: A South Asian Perspective

EXECUTIVE SUMMARY

There is no agreed definition of radicalization, and it has often been used pejoratively when talking about security in the West, Middle East, South Asia and elsewhere. In contemporary international politics, the radicalization discourse unfurls against tensions and negotiations between nations in terms of counter-terrorism and national security needs. A major dilemma at the heart of this discourse is the fundamental gap between radicalization as a cause of 'terrorism' and the actual acts signified by the term 'radicalization'. This study shows that radicalization does not appear to be a necessary condition for terrorism. It also shows that the discourse on radicalization in South Asia and in the West is essentially focused on Islam, ignoring various other proponents that deserve attention. A discussion on South Asian Islam and Hinduism, and the Western interpretation of Islam, reveals a complex set of relations among the religions and the politics of identity. Hence, being a Muslim or a Hindu is just one attribute in the complex menu of identities available to most South Asians. The complex architecture of state and public policy responses to radical movements and the mosaic of different forms of extremism have created myriad dilemmas in the West. Three predominant models of radicalization, introduced by the governments of the US, the UK and the EU, have been analysed to understand the embedded dilemmas in the West. These models indicate that radicalization is neither a predictable nor a mechanical process. The response to radicalization becomes further complicated by the awkward task of the Western governments to promote Western values in the East. This study also shows that it would be far too simplistic to say that radicalization is caused by the absence of democracy. The memories of the Partition of India in 1947 and of the birth of Bangladesh in 1971 denote that simplifying and stereotyping any 'identity' with radicalism would be problematic. Finally, the radicalization discourse is able to influence front-end decisions about what conduct to criminalize, or politically motivated decisions under embryonic statutes, such as the material support to terrorism. Therefore, the contents of this study may stimulate closer attention, for policy-makers as well as academic analysts, to the widespread, multifaceted, and profoundly important phenomenon of radicalization in South Asia.

RESEARCH METHODOLOGY

This study takes the conceptual problems with the terms 'radicalization', 'extremism' and 'terrorism' as its starting points. There are no agreed definitions of these concepts, and they have often been used pejoratively when talking about security in the West, Middle East, South Asia and elsewhere. This study limits its discussion on radicalization in the context of political economy of religion and extremism. By studying the literatures on radicalization, this research studies the impact of radicalization on contemporary regional security in South Asia. It should be noted that opacity about the sources of knowledge has hindered the research process. The manner in which oral knowledge is derived in South Asia has influenced conclusions. The range of methods for collecting materials (interviews, secondary materials such as published, unpublished material) proved to be particularly valuable in sharpening perspectives. Note was taken of the contrast between self-describing material and that emanating from others, including scholarly interpretations. The comparative perspective on the issue of radicalization has proved to be particularly revealing and instructive. Specifically, the comparative perspective has provided important avenues for developing the theoretical dimension of this study. In conformity with the research plan, extensive field visits were carried out in Bangladesh and India. The researcher is conversant with the Western discourse on radicalization due to his studies and research in the UK and other European countries in recent years. During field visits, numerous primary and secondary sources in Bengali and English were collected, and multiple interviews were conducted.

SCOPE OF THE PAPER

Although radicalization has increasingly been subjected to scientific studies, a universally accepted approach to theorize the concept is yet to be developed. Scientific and policy-related interest in the causal factors of radicalization has resulted in numerous efforts to define and shape the presumed pathways towards radicalism. Based on the literatures on radicalization, this study seeks to examine the most prominent causal factors of radicalization noticeable in the Western and South Asian discourses. In past and present studies, factors or conditions that are frequently mentioned as causes of radicalization (in general) include relative deprivation (Gurr 1970), Western occupations and support for oppressive regimes (Pape 2006), identity issues (Choudhury 2007), poor political and socio-economic integration (Veldhuis & Staun 2009), feelings of humiliation (Veldhuis & Staun 2009), and other psychological factors (Victoroff 2005). Although all these factors may contribute to radicalization, none suffices independently to explain the idea of radicalization. It should be noted, however, that radicalization literature is not a product of disinterested groups of experts, but has emerged in the context of local and transnational political economies. Internationally, it unfolds against tensions and negotiations between nations in both counter-terrorism and other security needs (Huq 2010).

This study does not aim to give an all-encompassing account of the factors that can be linked with radicalization. Rather, by taking stock of the literature from various disciplines, including socio-psychology, political economy, history and international relations, this study summarizes the most frequently used approaches on how terrorism, radicalization, and other related forms of behaviour come into being in different socio-economic settings. Therefore, its aim is twofold. First, it seeks to understand the similarities and differences in the Western and Eastern interpretations of radicalization. Second, it aims to answer the following research questions:

- Should 'radicalization' be understood as a response to statist policies towards minorities along with a spectrum of political or religious views?
- What could be the causal factors, in light of Eastern and Western discourses, that contribute to the process of radicalization in South Asia?

To sketch a comprehensive picture of how causal factors can lead to radicalization, a pragmatic framework of analysis has been introduced. This framework assumes that politics and religion are interdependent in shaping the circumstances under which radicalization is more or less likely to occur. The cases of Islamic radicalization in South Asia and Europe have been analysed. This framework, therefore, can be used to examine other types of radicalization, such as left-wing or right-wing extremism. Further, this study limits itself within the geographical territories of Bangladesh, India and Pakistan and within the politics involving the religions of Islam and Hinduism.

CHAPTER TWO

The Idea of Radicalization

UNDERSTANDING RADICALIZATION

Radicalization has emerged as an important phenomenon in contemporary discourse on terrorism, generating vast amounts of social, economic and political literatures. Analytical debate on terrorism is increasingly evolving around the concept of radicalization. This in turn has spawned research on the factors driving 'de-radicalization' and, conversely, 're-radicalization'. Yet, one of the main puzzles at the centre of such phenomena is the fundamental gap between radicalization as a cause of 'terrorism' and the actual acts signified by the term 'radicalization'. Despite the enormous resources that governments, for instance, devote to combating terrorism and extremism through deradicalization initiatives, the actual risks to the vast majority of those on whose behalf such activities are undertaken have never been statistically significant. For the purpose of this study, the central analytical task lies in 'explaining how such a small set of behaviours by small numbers of individuals generates a pervasive, intrusive and complex series of effects across the world' (Breen, Gunning, Jackson et al. 2008).

Much of the complexity in understanding radicalization derives from the widely held viewpoint among terrorism experts and counter-terrorism practitioners that terrorism depends on the radicalization of its instigators and perpetrators. For example, the UK Ministry of Justice and Home Office fears 'the potential of high-profile terrorist prisoners to radicalize susceptible imprisoned youths' (Pantucci 2008). Similarly, Sageman (2007) notes that 'the understanding of this process of radicalization is critical to assessing the threat facing the West and should be the basis guiding our interventions to counter it'. However, for all the attention the term has received, there has been meagre effort to define it. As Neumann (2008) put it, after 9/11, the term 'radicalization' entered the discourse to refer loosely to 'what goes on before the bomb goes off'. Neumann's comment was offered in the introductory chapter of a report entitled 'Perspectives on Radicalization and Political Violence', published by the International Centre for the Study of Radicalization and Political Violence (ICSR). It is worth noting that no definition of radicalization was provided in the various chapters of that report.

ICSR, however, is certainly not alone. Currently, there is no definition by the North Atlantic Treaty Organization (NATO) of the term 'radical' or any of its derivatives, such as radicalism or radicalization (NATO SA 2007). There are also no United Nations (UN) or European Union (EU) definitions of the term 'radicalization'. In fact, the *Concise Oxford English Dictionary* does not provide a definition of 'radicalization', 'radicalism', or even 'radicalize'.[1] What has become evident, however, is that radicalization, by most accounts, creates the motivational or cognitive preconditions ripe for terrorism. It would appear, therefore, that the implicit assumptions about radicalization are well grounded, suggesting that the states and agencies view radicalization as a 'process'.

Further, the term 'radicalization' becomes problematic in terms of its relationship to 'radicalism' as an expression of legitimate political thought. Radicalism as advocacy of, and commitment to, sweeping change and restructuring of political and social institutions has historically been associated with left- and right-wing political

[1] 'radical, *a.*' *The Oxford English Dictionary* (2nd edn., 1989), *OED Online*, Oxford: Oxford University Press. Also see, 'radical, *a.* and *n.*' *Oxford English Dictionary Additions Series* (1993), *OED Online*, Oxford: Oxford University Press. It does, however, list these terms as derivatives of *radical*. The relevant adjectival definitions of that latter include '(1) relating to or affecting the fundamental nature of something; (2) advocating thorough or complete political or social reform; politically extreme'. The relevant noun definition is '(1) an advocate of radical political or social reform'.

parties—at times even with centrist and liberal ideologies—and involves the wish to do away with traditional and procedural restrictions that support *status quo*. As an ideology, radicalism challenges the legitimacy of established norms and policies but does not, by itself, lead to violence. Several radical groups in South Asian political history have been reformist rather than revolutionary. In other words, there can be radicalism—without the advocacy of violence—to strive for the realization of social or political change.

Notwithstanding the growing consideration of radicalization as a precursor to terrorism—perhaps even a 'root cause' of terrorism and socio-political violence—it is widely agreed that, though radicalization increases the potential for different forms of violence, it does not necessitate any of them. For instance, according to a recent Global Futures Forum (GFF) report, 'radicalization is a process, not an end unto itself, and it does not necessarily lead to violence' (GFF 2006). This suggests that radicalization may not be a persuasive *vera causa* of terrorism because most radicals are not terrorists. This further implies that the term 'violent radicalization' often appears in discourse on terrorism due to limitation in defining radicalization (Huq 2010). If violence were indeed enforced by radicalization, the qualified term 'violent' would simply be redundant. Prevalent usage of terms such as 'violent radicalization' or 'militant radicalization' would thus seem to suggest that many theorists do not view radicalization as a sufficient cause of terrorism or other forms of violence (Neumann 2008). Therefore, radicalization is not a unified and linear concept (Huq 2010). Rather, there is an accumulation of dilemmas that may be associated with radicalization in different situations.

Radicalization does not appear to be an enabling condition for terrorism either. If the process of radicalization is regarded primarily as a psycho-social one, then acts of terrorism that are the products of strategic choice would appear to demonstrate that radicalization is unnecessary for terrorism to occur (Silber & Bhatt 2007). It remains an open question of how to appropriately characterize the relationship among radicalization, extremism, and terrorism without being subject to fallacious forms of cogitation wherein radicalization is seen as the root cause of terrorism. The notion that radicalization is in some sense a root cause of terrorism presumably has to do with something more than the fact that it derives from the Latin term *radix* meaning 'root' (Mandel, in press). However, for the purpose of this study, a working definition can be introduced: Radicalization entails a process of endorsing an extremist belief system and a method to perturb political and societal change(s). This definition separates radicalization from terrorism by emphasizing the interplay between radical actors and the institutions. Radical actors are individuals or communities and sub-populations experiencing radicalization. Institutions, hence governance and public policy, are the conduits facilitating or supporting an individual or a group through the radicalization process. They may be political institutions, transnational communities, influential leaders, historic documents, or even collective experiences or memories.

THE RADICALIZATION DISCOURSE IN SOUTH ASIA: HISTORICAL PERSPECTIVE

Western discourse on radicalization in South Asia is generally concentrated on radical Islam and has tended to focus on the Arab world, and the effects of this phenomenon on the West. There has been little discussion on the South Asian region except for a few debates, related more to Al-Qaeda terrorism and focused on 'fundamentalism' in Afghanistan, Pakistan and, in part, India. This discourse, to a greater extent, overlooked that the poorest and the largest number of Muslims live in the South Asian subcontinent, totalling around 480 million in three countries—India, Pakistan and Bangladesh (Sood & Kurginyan 2011). However, Islamic militancy was already a burning issue in much of the world by the end of the twentieth century. In late 2001, it quite unexpectedly hurtled to the top of the world threat list, driven by the terrorist attacks on New York and Washington, DC, and the subsequent global War on Terrorism (WoT). The humiliating defeat of Baathist-ruled Iraq by American-led coalition forces in April 2003 seemed bound to keep it there. Notwithstanding strenuous efforts in this period by numerous national leaders and a host of intellectuals to draw a clear distinction between Islam as a major and humane world religion and Islam as a cloak for politically motivated terrorist violence, the temptation to dilute the distinction has faced increasingly less resistance (Wirsing 2004). Regardless of the regions, Islam, whether combined rhetorically with militancy, fundamentalism, radicalism, or terrorism, without doubt currently occupies the spotlight in the West's efforts to beat back the current challenge to its dominance of the global order. Admittedly, Islam may persist in this role—or even fill it in catastrophically more violent ways—well into the future.[2] It should not be imagined, however, that Islam is the only religion on the planet able and willing to swell the ranks of religious radicalism or, for that matter, to inspire acts of terrorism.

Historically, until the decline of the Mughal empire in the eighteenth century, Muslim rulers presided over South Asian kingdoms and the majority of their subjects were Hindus. The exigencies of Muslim ascendancy in a non-Muslim environment demanded religious tolerance by the rulers and resulted in syncretism in the religion as practised by local Muslims. Unlike the Middle East, enforcement of the *shariah* in historic India was never complete. But Muslim *ulema*, *muftis* and *qazis* as well as laymen enjoyed a position of relative prestige as co-religionists of the rulers. The rise of British rule, culminating in the formal addition of India to the British empire after 1857, marked the end of this privileged position. The Muslim community's response to the gradual decline in Muslim political power came in the form of revivalist movements seeking to sharpen an Islamic identity. South Asia's Islamist political movements, therefore, trace their inspiration to Sheikh Ahmed Sirhindi's challenge in the sixteenth century to the ecumenism of Mughal emperor Akbar (Taylor 2010).

As a response to the failed 1857 Mutiny against the British by rebel Indian regiments in 1857, the Deoband was created. The 1857 Mutiny or, as it is known in India, the First War of

[2] This is the unsettling message of a recent commentary by James Kurth, a leading American academic in the field. According to Kurth (2002), 'a dialectical and symbiotic connection, perhaps an escalating and vicious cycle, exists between the growth of the American empire and the growth of Islamic terrorism and the world is about to witness a titanic and explosive struggle between them'.

Independence was brutally suppressed by the British. The Mutiny had also been vicious in its method, killing several colonial women and children it encountered. In revenge, the British laid waste to much of northern India, burning villages and leaving hundreds of people strung up from trees along the main highway. Lacking a clear strategy and credible leadership, the rebel soldiers had placed at the Mutiny's head the ageing and wholly titular last Mughal emperor, Bahadur Shah Zafar. Partly as a result, the British blamed Muslims more than others for the Mutiny and targeted the symbols of Islam in the reprisals that followed. Parts of Mughal Delhi were destroyed or vandalized; the city's great Jama Masjid—the largest mosque in India—became a camping ground for one of the Sikh regiments that had helped the British defeat the rebels. Prominent Muslim nobles and rebels remained in hiding for years. For them, it was a time for despair. The suppression of the Mutiny was an emphatic and crushing finale to the era of Islamic dynasties in India. India's Muslim intelligentsia was deeply split over how to respond. One group, led by Sir Sayyid Ahmad Khan, saw reconciliation as the only practical option. But Sir Sayyid's decision to make an accommodation with the British was also motivated by his fear of what would happen to Muslims in an independent India with a Hindu-majority population. His expectations of democracy in India were bleak: 'It would be a game of dice, in which one man had four dice and the other man one' (Luce 2006).

In the nineteenth century, the first *jihadi* group emerged in India and operated in the country's north-west frontier, including parts of present-day Pakistan and Afghanistan. This puritanical militant movement fought the region's Sikh rulers. The rise of British power simply changed the militants' target. The movement's founder, Sayyid Ahmed of Bareilly, organized cells throughout India to supply the frontier movement with men and money. Calling themselves *mujahideen*, the movement's followers interpreted the Islamic concept of *jihad* in its literal sense of 'holy war'. Sayyid Ahmed of Bareilly (not to be confused with Sir Sayyid Ahmad Khan) had been influenced by the ideas of Muhammad ibn-Abdul Wahhab, to which he had been exposed during his pilgrimage to Mecca. He called for a return to early Islamic purity and the reestablishment of Muslim political power. Sayyid Ahmed's revival of the ideology of *jihad* became the prototype for subsequent Islamic militant movements in South and Central Asia and is also the main influence over the *jihad* network of Al-Qaeda and its associated groups in the region (Haqqani 2005a).

The influence of Sayyid Ahmed's ideas and practices on South Asian Islamists is still visible in recent *jihad* literature in Pakistan, which invariably draws parallels between British colonial rule in the nineteenth century and US domination since the end of the twentieth century. Unlike in Sayyid Ahmed's time, today's jihad battlefield is not limited to a single geographic area (Taylor 2010). Despite the differences in technology and economy, the nineteenth-century *mujahideen* remain role models for today's *jihadis*, who make up an international network aimed at waging holy war at a time when the majority of Muslims seek to synthesize their faith with modern living. However, the revivalist ideas of Sheikh Ahmed Sirhindi and the *jihadi* ideology of Sayyid Ahmed of Bareilly alone do not explain the rise of modern *jihadis*. Even the large number of South Asian Muslims who embraced Western learning under British rule were influenced by revivalist ideas to the extent of seeking a separate identity for South Asia's Muslims, a process somewhat accelerated by the demand for and creation of Pakistan.

The emergence of Pakistan as an independent state in 1947 was a culmination of decades of debate and divisions among Muslims in British India about their collective future. In fact, Puritans like the Deobandis disapproved the idea of Pakistan, first raised in the 1930s. As a separate nation state, Pakistan was seen as a divisive prospect since it would artificially split the Ummah or community of believers. The concept of a Muslim-majority Pakistan rested on the notion that India's Muslims constituted a separate nation from non-Muslim Indians. Although the Islamists did not like the Westernized leadership that sought Pakistan and, in some cases, actively opposed the campaign for Pakistan, the lack of religious orthodoxy among Pakistan's founders did not prevent them from seeking the revival of Islam's lost glory in South Asia. In fact, the creation of a Muslim-majority state provided them with a better environment to pursue their ideas (Cohen 2004). Soon after independence, Pakistan's Constituent Assembly declared in 1949 that South Asian Muslims had created Pakistan for the principal objective of 'ordering their lives in accordance with the teachings and requirements of Islam' (Haqqani 2005a). Prominent individuals within the government mooted proposals for adopting Arabic as the national language, and of changing the script of the Bengali language from its Sanskrit base to an Arabic-Persian one. The president of the ruling Muslim League announced that Pakistan would bring all Muslim countries together into 'Islamistan'—a pan-Islamic entity. In 1949, the Pakistan government also sponsored the World Muslim Conference presided over by the Grand Mufti of Palestine, Amin al-Husseini, to promote Pan-Islamism. This conference led to the formation of the Motamar al-Alam al-Islami (Muslim World Congress), which has since played a crucial role in building up the feeling of Muslim victimization that has subsequently fed the global Islamist movement (Haqqani 2005b).

Since the creation of Pakistan, Islamist groups have been sponsored and supported by Pakistan's state machinery at different times to influence domestic politics and shore up Pakistani national identity, which is periodically threatened by sub-national ethnic challenges. The Islamists have also helped support the Pakistan military's political dominance. Islamists have been allies in the Pakistan military's efforts to seek 'strategic depth' in Afghanistan—a euphemism for Pakistan's efforts to make Afghanistan a client state of Pakistan—and to put pressure on India for negotiations over the future of Kashmir, the Muslim-majority Himalayan region that has been disputed by India and Pakistan since Partition. Pakistan's state institutions, notably national security institutions such as the military and the intelligence services, have played leading roles in building Pakistani national identity based on religion since Pakistan's emergence. This political commitment to an 'ideological state' gradually evolved into a strategic commitment to the *jihadi* ideology, especially during and after the Bangladesh war of 1971. Then, the Pakistan military used the Islamist's idiom and the help of Islamist groups to keep elected secular leaders supported by the majority Bengali-speaking population out of power (Haqqani

2005b). A Bengali rebellion and brutal suppression of the Bengalis by the military followed until the Great Liberation War of 1971 came into force.

During the 1971 war, Pakistan was divided, leading to the birth of independent Bangladesh. Until 1971, in West Pakistan, the effort to create national cohesion between Pakistan's divergent ethnic and linguistic groups through religion considerably impacted on East Pakistan and its manifestations became gradually militant. Religious groups, both militant and non-militant, gradually gained power because of this alliance between the mosque and the military. Radical and violent manifestations of Islamist ideology, which sometimes appear to threaten Pakistan's stability as well, are a state project gone wrong, in some ways. Given Pakistan's status as an ideological state, Islamic political groups of all kinds have proliferated in the country and several have received state patronage at one time or another. Others have operated independently or with the support of fellow Islamist groups outside the country. Meanwhile, for many Indians, the very existence of Pakistan is seen as a dagger aimed at the heart of India. This threat is perceived at multiple levels. First, Pakistan claims Kashmir, India's only Muslim majority province. Pakistan is unlikely to relinquish that claim, precisely because it is a Muslim-majority region (Luce 2006). If the so-called 'two-nation theory' is wrong, then Pakistan should never have been created.[3] If it is right, then Kashmir should belong to Pakistan. Given the degree to which Pakistan's military regimes have demanded national sacrifice in both blood and capital in pursuit of the Kashmir cause, it would be surprising if Islamabad abandoned its stance. Second, the creation of Pakistan has been seen as an amputation of India's natural geographical and cultural boundaries. It is not only Hindu nationalists who dream of a day

[3] The two-nation theory, that led to the birth of Pakistan in 1947, is an ideology that indicates that the primary identity of Muslims in the Indian subcontinent is Islam, rather than their language or ethnicity. It further signifies that the Indian Hindus and Muslims are two distinct nationalities, regardless of ethnic or other commonalities. The ideology that religion is the determining factor in defining the nationality of Indian Muslims is also a source of inspiration to several Hindu nationalist organizations. Also see Akbar (2003).

when Pakistan will be reincorporated into *Akhand Bharat* (Greater India). Many Indians, regardless of their social, ethnic or religious background, see the 1947 Partition as an unnecessary tragedy that ought, at some unspecified stage in the future, to be peacefully rectified. Naturally, this attitude contributes to Pakistan's own profound insecurities. However, very few Indians would any longer subscribe to Nehru's view that Pakistan was untenable as a nation state and that would eventually merge back into India. Indian longing for subcontinental unity remains a vague sentiment (Nehru 1946; Azad 1988). Third, and most intractably, Pakistan is seen as posing an existential threat to India's secular identity.

Over and above the 'passionate hatred' between India and Pakistan, the narration of history at school levels has emerged as a disturbing element (Luce 2006).[4] According to Pakistan's school textbooks, the history of modern Pakistan goes back to the early Muslim incursions into India, when marauders such as Mahmood Ghazni, an Afghan strongman, conducted raids on northern India. Pakistan's medium range nuclear missiles are called Ghauri, after Mohammed Ghauri, who became the first Muslim to rule Delhi when he defeated a Hindu Rajput prince, Prithviraj Chauhan, in 1192. Meanwhile, India's short range missiles are called Prithvis (*prithvi* also means 'earth' in Sanskrit). In a mirror image of the textbooks that the Bharatiya Janata Party (BJP) introduced when it governed India, Pakistan's schoolbooks stereotype Hindus as 'cunning, scheming and deceptive'. The textbooks used in the 20,000-plus schools operated by the Hindu nationalist Rashtriya Swayamsevak Sangh (RSS) in India depict Muslims as cruel and bloodthirsty. Further, Emperor Aurangzeb, is depicted as a hero by Pakistan but as a villain by India. His greatgrandfather, Akbar, one of India's most enlightened rulers, is downplayed by both Muslim and Hindu communalists. They are two sides of the same coin (Luce 2006).

Meanwhile, the birth of Bangladesh in 1971, apparently in the name of Bengali nationalism, signalled the departure of 'political Islam' or the Islam-based state ideology of the Pakistan

[4] See Desai (2005) for an elaboration of the term 'passionate hatred'.

period (1947–71). To some scholars, the creation of Bangladesh delegitimized the two-nation theory, which in 1947 justified the communal Partition of the Indian subcontinent into India and Pakistan. Soon after its emergence, Bangladesh adopted the four-pronged state ideology of nationalism, democracy, socialism and secularism. However, not long after the emergence of the nation state, Islam re-emerged as an important factor in the country, both socially and politically. Although the not-so-democratic regime of Sheikh Mujibur Rahman (1972–5) retained secularism along with democracy, socialism and nationalism as the state principles, his assassination and the overthrow of his government by a military *coup d'état* in August 1975 brought in Islam-oriented state ideology by shunning secularism and socialism. Not long after his ascendancy as the new ruler in November 1975, General Ziaur Rahman replaced the outwardly secular 'Bengali nationalism' with 'Bangladeshi nationalism'. One may argue that 'Bangladeshi' is inclusive of the different non-Bengali minorities; nevertheless, the term highlights the Muslim identity of the country, differentiating its Muslim majority Bengalis from their Hindu majority counterparts in West Bengal in India (Hashmi 2004).

It is interesting to note that despite the constant harping on the themes of Islamic solidarity and Muslim separatism under the aegis of the Pakistani ruling classes during 1947 and 1971, most East Bengali Muslims distanced themselves from 'communal/political Islam'. Not long after the Partition of 1947, East Bengali Muslims started to prefer secular institutions, including democracy, over Islam for the sake of their Bengali identity. The clash of these two identities—'Islamic' (Pakistani) and 'secular' (Bengali)—also catalysed the creation of Bangladesh (Kamal 1989). During 1971–5, Bengali nationalism, or more precisely East Bengali nationalism, had been the guiding principle of the then Awami League government. However, for the top leaders and bulk of the followers, Bengali nationalism only meant linguistic and other aspects of culture, excluding religion. This means they were (are) Bengalis but nevertheless remained (remain) Muslims at the same time. However, the rulers of the new nation of Bangladesh for various reasons—mainly political—adopted the four-pronged state ideology of 'Bengali nationalism', socialism, secularism and democracy, a la Nehruvian 'democratic socialism' (often touted as 'Mujibism'). The abysmal failure of Mujibism and the one-party system through the Bangladesh Peasants' and Workers' Awami League (BKSAL) to alleviate poverty and restore law and order eventually led to the Islamization of the polity.

In the long run, Islamic parties outpaced various secular/leftist parties in the wake of the overthrow of the BKSAL regime in August 1975. Subsequently, both military and civil governments of the country promoted political Islam to contain the militant one promoted by the grassroots-based, well-organized Jamaat-i-Islami and other groups. It is noteworthy that General Zia's government (1975–81) withdrew the ban imposed on all Islam-oriented political parties by the Mujib government for their active collaboration with the Pakistani occupation forces in 1971. Zia and his successors promoted Islam and Islamic parties, including the Jamaat and Muslim League, for the sake of legitimacy and for containing the most organized Awami League (Hashmi 1994). However, after the fall of General Zia's government, General Hussain Muhammad Ershad took over the power in 1981 and amended the constitution in June 1988 by introducing Islam as the state religion.

One may argue that General Ershad, of all people, could not be sincere about his commitment to Islam. He played the Islamic card for the sake of containing the so-called fundamentalist forces and his secular opponents by legitimizing his rule among most Bangladeshi Muslims who, according to a study, favour non-cleric, English-educated, 'anti-Indian' and Islam-oriented politicians as their leaders. The 1991 parliamentary elections, held after the overthrow of Ershad in December 1990, brought Khaleda Zia, President Zia's widow, to power. Her Bangladesh Nationalist Party (BNP) came to power with support from the Jamaat-i-Islami and she became the prime minister. It is interesting that most political parties, including the Communist Party of Bangladesh, used Islamic slogans for their success in the elections of 1991. While the 'pro-Islamic' parties got 54.13 per cent of the votes, the Awami League-led eight-party alliance, despite its Islamic rhetoric, slogans and banners, managed to poll only around 34.81 per cent of the votes in the elections (Hashmi 1994).

This discussion reveals complex relations between Muslims and Hindus, as well as between Pakistan and India, and generates several observations. A critical observation is that radical departure from pluralism to religious extremism often involves a search for identity at a moment of crisis or the interests of the religious elites to secure 'power'. Such crises create a 'cognitive opening', a moment when an individual or a group finds that the existing structure of the society and the state, and certainly their belief system, is inadequate to decipher their experiences. This means that the identity crisis is a sense of alienation from the society or the socio-economic existence. The intensity of such alienation is reinforced by experiences of deprivation and discrimination, a sense of censorship in social mobility, and a lack of confidence in the political system. As a part of this process, individuals resort to construct an identity in the face of globalization. Further, the socio-psychology of extremist groups reflects, in part, the deficiency in existing religious institutions and organizations to address their questions, concerns and grievances.

THE CONTINUUM SYNDROME

Nehru (1946) once described India as a palimpsest. It was his way of illustrating the large accumulation of histories and cultures that left their mark on the country, and were never fully erased. The patterns of radicalization, which have stemmed extremist movements in South Asia, active since the Mughal era (and United India), can be classified into four groups. The first is centred on the Jamaat-e-Islami founded by Islamist scholar Maulana Abul Ala Maududi in 1941. The second includes the Deobandi movements that arose from the austere interpretations of Islam by the Deoband *madrasa* founded in 1867 to protect Muslims from being seduced by Western materialism. The third group of South Asian jihadists is 'Wahhabi', influenced by the doctrine of Muhammad ibn-Abdul Wahhab and almost invariably funded by Saudi Arabia. These three groups, whether actively or not, will continue their presence by the virtue of their embedded roots in the South Asian society. The fourth group is that of Hindu nationalists that coalesced at the all-India level since the Partition of 1947.

While Islamist extremist movements remain factors of influence in Bangladesh and Pakistan, the RSS has emerged as the central organization of nationalist ideological tendency, and its relationship to political parties and other organizations associated with Hindu nationalism. The enduring tension in Hindu nationalism between organizational loyalty and ideological purity sustains as a critical factor in Indian ethno-religious politics. Hindu nationalism, which for so long existed on the margins of Indian political life, came to dominate the polity fifty years after Independence. The argument is that the ideological factors often cited as reasons for the growth of the BJP—the broadcast of Hindu epics during the Congress period of the 1980s, and the movement to replace a mosque at Ayodhya with a temple—with the connivance of the Congress, played a permissive role at best. The growth of the BJP has occurred not as a direct result of these factors but because of its ability to exploit material and status grievances among discrete segments of Indian society, as well as rivalries within Congress party and between the Congress and various regional parties. While most of these issues had a natural affinity with traditional positions of Hindu nationalists, the affinity was not due to a religious agenda but due to a militaristic approach to foreign policy, a historic preference for smaller states (to strengthen the central government), and their traditional opposition to affirmative action. Therefore, being a Muslim or being a Hindu is just one attribute in the complex menu of identities available to most South Asians.

CHAPTER THREE

The Contemporary Religious Landscape in South Asia

MISSING LINKS: NEW CHANGES AND CHALLENGES IN THE RELIGIOUS LANDSCAPE

It is a well-documented fact that the understandings of the religious are often coloured by misperception, if not by myth. There is also a great deal of misperception and mythologizing among external observers about Islam and Muslims. This is, in most cases, the result of complex historical, sociological and political factors (Azra 2005). The history of Islam in South Asia indicates that the South Asian version of Islam is among the least Arabicized forms of Islam. It is generally peaceful and gradual, and essentially influenced by Sufism. However, a purer and orthodox form of Islam has simultaneously and steadily penetrated deeper into parts of the region. By the end of the Cold War, globalization brought a move towards Islamic rejuvenation that can be observed clearly among Muslims in South Asia, particularly in India, Bangladesh and Pakistan, over the past two decades. This rejuvenation brought new tendencies in religious observance as well as new institutions and new Muslim groups; new Islamic lifestyles have increasingly been adopted by many Muslims in this period. New mosques with new architecture (usually derived from the Middle East) have been constructed—and they are full of congregations, mostly youthful. At the same time, more and more Muslims have performed the Hajj, the pilgrimage to Mecca. In fact, the number of pilgrims from South Asia (approximately 225,000 Muslims per annum) is the largest compared to those coming from other areas of the

Muslim world. At the same time, an increasingly large sum of religious alms and donations (*zakat*, *infaq* and *sadaqah*) have been collected from well-to-do Muslims and distributed among the poor and deprived Muslims. New banking systems have been introduced, like the Islami Bank Bangladesh Ltd., which has been phenomenally successful.[1]

However, four fundamental and interdependent yet contradictory driving forces are active behind this process of change in the structure of South Asian religions. One of the forces is the global WoT launched in October 2001. The WoT has had a visibly profound impact on the states of South Asia—on Pakistan most directly and physically, of course, but in one way or another on the others as well. Its impact on these states has been, in certain key respects, less traumatic—less politically and socially destabilizing—than in the case of countries in some other regions. This is in part because South Asia, so far at least, has not been a primary target in the war. It housed none of the so-called 'rogue' states, none of the notorious 'axis of evil'. In the larger part, the states of South Asia have taken the WoT more or less in their stride because religious radicalism and its terrorist offshoots were staples of their political agendas long before they reared their heads in New York and Washington, DC. This phenomenon does not project much novelty in South Asia. Indeed, few of the world's other geographic regions can boast of more deeply entrenched and widely felt patterns of religious radicalism than have been evident for decades in South Asia. This applies especially to the two largest and most populous countries in the region (India, Pakistan) but also, albeit to a lesser extent, to Bangladesh. Though these states differ greatly amongst themselves, the root, nature and scale of religion-related radicalism in all three are now major public issues. They crop up

[1] This banking system is also known as shari'ah banks, since they operate in accordance with Islamic law. Besides, the Islamic insurance (*takaful*) system is gradually gaining popularity in the region. Now, several large banks, such as HSBC and Standard Chartered also maintain Shari`ah divisions or branches.

constantly both in domestic politics and in their relations with one another.

The second force is the steadily emerging economic connect between the Wahhabi states and South Asia. The Wahhabi doctrine, a puritanical version of Islamic reformism, has the capacity to fuel Islamist radicalism in the region (Ahmed 2005). The very strict and orthodox Wahhabi brand of Islam was founded by Muhammad Ibn al-Wahhab (*c.* 1703–91) and rejects all Islamic practices adopted after the third century of the Muslim era (approximately CE 950).[2] The growth of the Wahhabi sect around the world can be explained via two reasons. First, the sect markets itself as the 'purest' brand of Islam. Second, it has been patronized by the Saudi royal family, the Saudi Arabian government, and especially Saudi-based charities, which have financed thousands of Islamic schools, including Qw'ami *madrasas*, around the world. The financial power of Saudi Arabia has ensured that its predominant Islamic sect has been able to propagate itself, including in regions such as South Asia, that have always had very tolerant and broad interpretations of Islam. The Jamaat-e-Islami and other Islamist parties have been advocating a stricter, more intolerant brand of Islam and they condemn the secular nation state. They are at the core of a growing and powerful Islamic extremist movement and have established networks within South Asia and the Middle East. One cannot underestimate the influence of the ongoing conflict in the Middle East, which has a massive impact on popular opinion in Bangladesh and beyond. While the Palestinian issue is primarily a national struggle, it strikes a chord in the Muslim world. The injustice suffered by Palestinians has become a metaphor for the injustices borne by all Muslims, while the Americans, already scapegoats for the region's security woes, are implicated yet again (Khan 2010).

[2] Wahhab considered it a duty to conquer all other 'heretical' sects of Islam practised among the Saudi tribes. He allied himself with one clan, the Saud, in 1744. In the mid-1760s, the Saud completed their conquest of Saudi Arabia and, ever since, there have been close links between the House of Saud and the Wahhabi sect.

The third force is the emergence of new and high-quality Islamic educational institutions—parallel to the mainstream education and contrary to the Qw'ami *madrasas*—in Bangladesh, India and Pakistan. These are established either by Muslim private foundations or by the state. In Bangladesh, this includes the Islamic University set up by the Government of Bangladesh and numerous other Islamic universities and colleges. India hosts the region's oldest Islamic university, the Aligarh Muslim University. These Islamic higher educational institutions undoubtedly play an important role in the modernization of Muslim society. Owing much to 'rational' and 'non-denominational' approaches to Islam, graduates of these universities in general have been recognized by South Asian societies as having progressive, inclusive and tolerant views of Islam. Many students and graduates of mainstream (meaning secular) universities tend to be more literal in their view and understanding of Islam. Graduates of the Islamic universities are increasingly becoming instrumental in the building and spread of Islamic institutions such as the Islamic schools, modern *madrasas*, NGOs and *majlis ta'lim* (religious group discussions in offices and society at large). Meanwhile, many new quality schools and *madrasas* have also been established since the late 1980s. It is inaccurate to assume that in Bangladesh and India, the *madrasas* and Islamic centres of education have become 'breeding grounds' of Talibanism or extremism, unlike many *madrasas* in Afghanistan or Pakistan (Khan 2010). Pakistan's reputation has been subjected to a relentless battering in recent years. Pakistan is routinely described in the Western media as a politically maimed and potentially 'failed' or 'failing' state. Pakistan was portrayed by responsible observers, even before 9/11, as 'drifting toward religious extremism' (Bearak 2001). Apparently, many Pakistan Army officers 'share the religious zeal of the fundamentalists' and the country's thousands of *madrasas* serve as massive institutional incubators of religious fanaticism as well as recruiting centres for the Islamic *jihad* (Ganguly 2000).

The fourth, but not the least, factor is the context of domestic politics and political economy of religion in the South Asian countries. Militant Hindu movements, not infrequently tinged with violence and terrorism, have lengthy histories in India.

Religious radicalism is not a rarity amongst Christians in the region and beyond, either.[3] On India's domestic front, religious radicalism has found its politically most powerful expression in the idea of Sangh Parivar—the family of militant Hindu groups (including, most notably, the RSS, the Vishwa Hindu Parishad [VHP], and the Bajrang Dal) that form the organizational backbone of contemporary Hindu nationalism. The Hindutva ideology of these groups, having the goal of a united Hindu Rashtra (Hindu Nation)—and asserting the existence of a blanket 'Hindu' national identity for all of India's inhabitants, be they formally Hindu or not—occupies one side in a heated and momentous debate over India's national destiny. Currently well-positioned to advance its Hindutva-oriented understanding of these is the BJP, the political embodiment of Hindu nationalism. For all of India's political parties, however, no matter how liberal and secular they claim to be, the matter of religious identity is never very far from the top of the political agenda. It is worth noting that, having survived for years on Western political agendas primarily as an instance of human rights deprivation, the Kashmir dispute now seemed in real danger of slipping into the category of just another front in the global WoT (Wirsing 2004).

It is indeed a fact that Hindutva has insistently and deliberately unravelled all the threads that were fashioned to knit a multi-linguistic, multi-religious India together; it pitted community against community, and destroyed spaces where people of different religious persuasions had learned to live together. After the Gujarat pogrom, an RSS meeting stated brazenly that minorities have to

[3] On the contrary, there are indications that the world's rapidly expanding Christian population may be acquiring 'fundamentalist' traits hitherto attributed mainly to Islam. Observing that 'in the past half century the critical centres of the Christian world have moved decisively to Africa, to Latin America, and to Asia', Pennsylvania State University historian Philip Jenkins argues that revolutionary change in world Christianity is in progress, that the motivation for change is conservative and fundamentalist at its core, and that 'in its variety and vitality, in its global reach, in its association with the world's fastest-growing societies, in its shifting centres of gravity, in the way its values and practices vary from place to place'.

gain the goodwill of the majority if they want to live in the country.[4] The VHP has gone a step further and stated that minorities should be condemned to living in refugee camps as they do in strife-torn Gujarat. What is more problematic is that members of the Hindutva brigade can terrorize minorities, deny them their rights, exterminate them—and the governments at the state and the centre will acquiesce by their silence. Hindutva can be read in many terms but it is mainly an ideology. Yet it is an ideology like no other, because it has relentlessly and insistently tapped the intangible and the incorporeal properties of the collective psyche of the Hindus in some deep and unfathomable way. It has excavated memories of 'Hindu' loss, of betrayal, and of humiliation, which had perhaps been buried under layers of other memories, and catapulted them into the open. To put it differently, the Hindutva agenda has been constructed along one main pivot: what psychiatrists call the 'recovered memory syndrome'.[5] Narrative after narrative coming from the Sangh Parivar speaks of the historical mortification of the majority community and of its current helplessness (Chandhoke 2001).

The Ayodhya case could be cited again. What is interesting is the way in which the narrative of Ayodhya was to constitute the

[4] Widespread killings, mostly of Muslims, were carried out with the apparent involvement of several ministers in the government itself, under the leadership of Bharatiya Janata Party Chief Minister Narendra Modi in 2002 in Gujarat. All available evidence, unusually well documented in the case of Gujarat, indicates beyond a shadow of doubt that the Sangh Parivar (the umbrella organization of all militant Hindu organizations) was well-prepared and well-rehearsed to carry out the murderous and brutal attacks on Muslim men, women, and children. The incident had direct linkages with local politics in Godhra; militant Hindu political movement centred around the demand for the building of a new temple to Lord Rama in the northern Indian town of Ayodhya; and with a post-pogrom intent on the part of the BJP government in Gujarat to take advantage of presumed Hindu political consolidation for electoral purposes, by calling for early state legislative assembly elections.

[5] Of course, not all Hindus feel this way, and many have protested and challenged the narrative. What counts is that the narrative has proved powerful because increasing numbers of the majority community subscribe to notions of historical victimhood.

site of the Babri mosque as double-coded memory. On the one hand, the site served to evoke memories of violation, destruction, desecration, and illegitimate occupation of sacred sites by Mughal rulers. It signified the chagrin of the Hindus even as they had watched helplessly as their temples had been destroyed and their Gods rendered homeless by the 'invader' in the past. On the other hand, as the site of the proposed Ramjanmabhoomi temple, Ayodhya became the referral of the proposed Hindu Rashtra. It simply represented a space where a mortified and outraged people would redeem history, erase memories of humiliation, recover religious institutions, and forge a future for the Hindus and by the Hindus. The narrative of Ayodhya, in other words, was a narrative that aspired to power in the near future; it was a narrative that was to prepare the ground in civil society for the control of the state by the forces of Hindutva. The attempt to control the future to repaint the past, and to repaint the past to control the future was manifest, even as the Ayodhya narrative rapidly and dexterously juxtaposed two narratives: narratives of shame and victimhood, and narratives of intent to reclaim history. And for this very purpose, the Ramjanmabhoomi narrative proclaimed a closure onto other memories of Ayodhya (Chandhoke 2001; Akbar 1988). For though the Sangh Parivar was to capitalize upon the Babri mosque/Ayodhya as memorializing humiliation, it is equally true that other narratives of and on Ayodhya existed in popular memory, through anecdotes, stories, and mythologies (Chandhoke 2001).

IMPLICATIONS OF THE CHANGES: RISE OF EXTREMIST ENTITIES

The implications of changes and the impact of historical discourse have demonstrated profound consequences on South Asia, irrespective of geographical boundaries, political stripes or governance models. For example, the implications could be understood by analysing the activities of the RSS, the VHP, and the Lashkar-e-Taiba (LeT). The cases of the Gujarat riots and the Moradabad pogrom could be cited here. The Gujarat riots, in which more than 1,000 Muslims were killed in a state-tolerated—

perhaps even state-sanctioned—revenge for the brutal slaying of fifty-eight Hindus, came as a considerable shock, both nationally and internationally. The BJP at the centre of these events had shelved the contentious issues that led to the 1993 Hindu–Muslim riots, and they always want to control their more radical Hindu partners in the country and beyond. India, after all, has the aspiration to become a regional, perhaps even global, power. In the wake of the Gujarat riots, many concluded that this was an optimistic assessment.

The BJP government at the centre might have put aside contentious issues, such as the campaign for a Hindu temple at the site of a mosque that Hindu radicals destroyed in 1992 (Babri Masjid),[6] but it was unable to restrain its radical wings in the states. The BJP-led Gujarat government revived the temple agitation when its allies tried to bury it; at the same time, Gujarat's extremist chief minister, Narendra Modi, made great play on Pakistan-backed terrorism in India. Gujarat's Hindus and Muslims were polarized, and one of Gujarat's former hot spots, Godhra, erupted when Hindu temple activists came to blows with local Muslims at the railway station. Muslim radicals set fire to a carriage-load of men, women and children, killing fifty-eight. Revenge riots broke out across Gujarat, many of them led by Hindu activists affiliated with the Gujarat government. The state government failed to stop the riots until more than 1,000 Muslims were killed, some literally torn apart. The Gujarat government's policy of 'turning a blind eye' to the carnage, and the central government's decision to opt for pressure on the state government instead of dismissing it and placing the state under Governor's rule, allowed more

[6] The campaign to build a temple to the widely worshipped Hindu figure Ram at the site of a seventeenth-century Muslim mosque in northern India was launched in the late 1980s. The mosque was destroyed by Hindu mobs in December 1992, fuelling Hindu–Muslim riots in western India (where extremist Hindu organizations such as the VHP and the Shiv Sena have a strong presence). When the BJP came to power at the centre in coalition with a number of regional parties, the temple campaign was put on the backburner, but when the BJP came to power in Gujarat under the leadership of Narendra Modi the campaign was revived—once again followed by Hindu–Muslim riots.

than 1,000 preventable deaths. Muslims continued to be harassed after the violence subsided. It looked as if India was beginning to undergo the same process of religious radicalization as so many of its neighbours—and with potentially worse consequences for its minorities, especially the 120-million-plus Indian Muslims (by virtue of scale). It is indeed a very tragic divorce of two communities, which used to be interlinked and overlapping. 'Now the Muslims of Gujarat are standing out and saying: "If you want us to be different, we will be different"' (Luce 2006). The Bush administration has been especially criticized by the international community for not having reacted to the Gujarat riot more strongly than it did. The Europeans, who had reacted strongly, were under pressure to do more. Were not the Hindu xenophobes of Gujarat on par with Islamic militants? (Kumar 2004) This is a question that the US and European administrations were asked, in parliament and by many civil society groups (especially in Britain where the Gujarati Muslim diaspora is strong).

Unlike in Gujarat, the population of Moradabad in Uttar Pradesh is divided almost equally between Hindus and Muslims. This should have had acted as a recipe for peace rather than violence, at least generally. On 13 August 1980, an astonishing incident of violence took place when the Provincial Armed Constabulary opened fire on about 40,000 Muslims while they were at their Eid prayers. An exact number of casualties could not be found. This incident at Moradabad was not a Hindu–Muslim riot but a calculated, cold-blooded massacre of Muslims by a rabidly communal police force, which tried to cover up its genocide by projecting it as a Hindu–Muslim communal clash (Akbar 1988). The situation was exploited by the BJP, which had lost the 1980 election and was trying to regain the political dominance in the area (Sharma 1996). The massacre gave signals that there is a growing impatience among the Hindus, and the evident rise of the feeling that the majority community is always undermined to favour the minorities for petty political gains. Therefore, the then Prime Minister Indira Gandhi, despite her promises, could not punish the Hindu policemen involved in this massacre. Subsequently, the Congress shifted its approach towards the minority communities. In the 1984 elections, for the first time, the Congress appealed to the caste Hindus that only it could protect the country from the threat posed by the minorities (Engineer 1991).

Similarly, outfits such as the LeT, which is religiously inspired and maintains a professionally guided Islamist agenda, emerged with the support of the Pakistan government. Translated literally as 'Army of the Pure/Righteous', the LeT is a radical, Pakistan-based Sunni Islamic group, which primarily operates in the disputed Jammu & Kashmir region. Founded in 1989, the LeT is said to be the militant wing of the Markaz Dawa wal Irshad (MDI), a Pakistan-based centre for religious instruction established in 1987. The LeT is reported to be a leading member of the International Islamic Front, which campaigns against the UK, the US, India, and Bangladesh. Its primary objective is to liberate Muslims in Jammu & Kashmir and make the region an Islamic state by incorporating it into Pakistan. It is also said to advocate action within and against countries with non-Islamic governments. The LeT, as it maintains longstanding ties to Islamabad's Inter-Services Intelligence (ISI), has emerged as a potential extremist group for inflaming regional tensions in South Asia. The group has been implicated in the December 2008 Mumbai attacks, which provoked further military tensions between India and Pakistan. The LeT's agenda aims at the destruction of 'Christian Crusaders and Jews' (Hindus have also been added to the list). A number of reports indicate that Pakistan's main intelligence agency, the ISI, continues to give the LeT intelligence help and protection. The LeT's vision includes establishing a pan-Islamic Caliphate but, since 9/11, its primary objective has remained the liberation of Kashmir and the destruction of India. For this reason, within Pakistani society and in the eyes of the state, the LeT's identity has remained separate from that of Al-Qaeda and other *jihadi* actors, enabling the group to position itself as the 'good *jihadis*'. Because of this the Pakistani state rewarded the LeT with preferential treatment, which the group leveraged during the first several years following 9/11 to provide (primarily) covert assistance to Al-Qaeda and other actors drawn to a global *jihadi* agenda.

All of these developments represent wider changes within South Asian Muslim communities, as well as non-Muslim communities. It indicates that, since the 1980s, a new Muslim middle class has developed. Although this new Muslim middle class is heavily tied to, and dependent upon, the ruling regimes in the respective countries, there is little doubt that they have played significant roles in the construction of, and in support of, the new Islamic institutions. Further, they are instrumental in the spread of new lifestyles, or even a new tradition of conducting religious discussions, seminars, and ceremonies in hotels and other prominent places. Hence, the complex architecture of state responses and the mosaic of different forms of extremism have created a multi-faceted dilemma in the West. Recourse to the use of terror by religious fundamentalists during the aforementioned changes was inevitable and is not historically unique. Fundamentalism degenerating into radicalism has not been a phenomenon of Islam alone. For nearly a century, Muslims and Hindus have been developing a militant form of piety, with the objective of dragging God and religion back to the centrestage from the sidelines, a position to which they had been relegated by modern secular culture (Sood 2011). 'These "extremists" (fundamentalists) as they are called, are convinced that they are fighting for the survival of their faith in a world turned hostile to religion' (Armstrong 2001). To most of the West and secular practitioners in South Asia, modernism is synonymous with freedom, liberation, human association and achievements but to the religious extremists, modernity—or, for that matter, change in the conventional system—is an invasion of their essential beliefs. The inspiration for the spread of extremism has come from state policies that sought refuge and utility in religion, and drew inspiration from puritan influences outside its own borders (Khan 2012).

Therefore, the puritanical agenda of the Islamist groups zeroes in on the growing strength of the intolerant fractions of societies as the principal threat. Because of the state failures in dealing with extremism, a growing number of radical, self-generating groups in South Asia will gradually dominate political institutions. The discussion under this section leads to a major analytic ambiguity regarding radicalization. The idea of radicalization in South Asia shows double structure, which posits a categorical linkage between that faith and political violence. In this fashion, neither the Western nor the South Asian discourses are 'mere unconditioned ratiocination' without preconditions because both discourses treat the 'Muslim' a priori as a source of risk and harm. This extends a long intellectual history that Edward Said has most famously excavated, a history based on 'the ineradicable distinction between Western superiority and Oriental inferiority' (Said 1979).

CHAPTER FOUR

Identifying the Causal Factors: The Process of Radicalization

THE STRUCTURE OF RADICALIZATION IN WESTERN DISCOURSE

The trends in the radicalization discourse in South Asia, as discussed in Chapters Two and Three, to a great extent contradict the conventional wisdom that poverty and economic failures are the causal reasons behind the rise and steady growth of radical ideologies and extremism. Part of the work of the radicalization discourse, therefore, tends to substantiate the claim that this is a statist problem stemming largely from the political economy of religion and failure of statist institutions. Radicalization literature also claims that ideology, including religious ideology, still plays a central role in the radicalization process. There is a need to move beyond an effort to disconnect religion from violence, and instead focus on empirical evidence that suggests that a *deficit* of religious knowledge presents a concern with respect to questions of radicalization. Professor Tufyal Choudhury pioneered this argument in an April 2007 paper for the UK government office for communities and local government (Choudhury 2007). He aggregated research about why people commit acts of violence, focusing on the role of religion. Examining studies of groups such as Al-Muhajiroun and Hizb-ut-Tahrir, Choudhury argued that research showed that 'the path to [radicalization] often involves a search for identity in a moment of crisis'. Whether because it is intrinsically belligerent or because it provides marginalized and disparaged communities with increased in-group solidarity, the identity of 'Muslim' has proven increasingly attractive in recent decades.

Quintan Wiktorowicz's pioneering study on the Salafist group Al-Muhajiroun indicates that those attracted to marginal religious groups 'are not particularly religious and do not have any significant religious education' and 'a lack of religious literacy and education appears to be a common feature among those that are drawn to extremist groups' (Choudhury 2007; Wiktorowicz 2005). Despite this uncertainty, the paper recommended, 'Muslims will be better equipped to counter violent [radicalization] when they have the knowledge and ideas about their faith with which to confront extremists'. In line with the case of Islamist radicalization, the radicalization of Hinduism and infusion of Hindu nationalism into India's politics is emerging as a divisive force that threatens India's secularism. Rahul Gandhi, the icon of the Indian National Congress, has said that, 'Hindu terror groups could pose a bigger threat to India than Muslim militant groups like the LeT' (Oneindia News 2010). A study identified that 'within India, Maoists pose a far greater threat than Muslim militants in 150 districts, one-third of India's area. However, major cities feel threatened only by Muslim groups. Therefore, the national elite and media focus overwhelmingly on Muslim terrorism. The elite are hardly aware that this is an elite phenomenon' (Aiyar 2001). Therefore, widespread stereotyping of Muslims, and in that matter of any religion, still remains a dominant factor among the policy-makers, leaders and among the elites.

IN SEARCH OF THE CAUSAL FACTORS: APOSTOLIC MODELS OF RADICALIZATION PROMULGATED BY THE WEST

The proportion of potentially radical individuals is so small and diverse that it is impossible to categorize them into groups with specified social boundaries. However, it could be predicted that social identification of the allegedly detrimental (extremist or perhaps terrorist) groups is an important indicator of vulnerability to radicalization. In particular, for people for whom group membership of the relevant group is central to the self-concept, threats of the group are likely to increase radicalization tendencies. However, to identify the causal factors in and social identity of radicalization and radicalized groups three different models were developed by the New York Police Department (NYPD), the UK Home Office, and the European Commission (EC). It could be noted that neither significant research nor models to interpret radicalization had been developed in South Asia. However, the models developed in the West became well-discussed by the state agencies, policy communities, and academics in South Asian countries. These models have significant impact on determining the bilateral relations of Bangladesh, India and Pakistan with countries like the US, the UK and the EU (henceforth referred as the West). A critical examination of these models developed would provide insights into the problems in understanding the South Asian process of radicalization.

Corresponding to the nature and structure of radicalization, the first and most prominent analysis of radicalization at the state level has been conducted in the US. The NYPD's Intelligence Division published *Radicalization in the West: The Homegrown Threat* in August 2007 (Silber & Bhatt 2007). The NYPD report's analytic ambition presents a larger aspiration. The authors used a broad scope, documenting ten case studies of alleged or completed terrorist conspiracies: five from Europe and Canada and five from the US. But the report has a narrow focus along a different axis: all ten case studies were linked explicitly or implicitly to Al-Qaeda. The sample population for the report comprised all terrorism incidents in the world, but the actual sample included only terrorism explicitly or notionally connected to Islam. Selection, clearly, was not random but directed by an interest in certain forms of terrorism. Elaborating these case studies, the report perceives a consistency in the radicalization process. The report proposes a socio-psychological model with four stages to the radicalization process, 'each with its distinct set of indicators and signatures' (Silber & Bhatt 2007). These are: (1) pre-radicalization, (2) self-identification, (3) indoctrination, and (4) jihadization (Silber

& Bhatt 2007). The four stages of radicalization act as a funnel according to the report: once a person enters, he or she might not reach 'jihadization' but will remain 'a threat' (Silber & Bhatt 2007). This has expansive consequences. Consider the definition of the 'pre-radicalization' phase stipulated by the report. Individuals are 'pre-radical', according to the NYPD's logic, when they live in geographic Muslim enclaves, which are 'ideological sanctuaries' for the 'seeds of radical thought'; when they are between 15- and 35-year-old males; and when they are middle class and educated through at least high school (Silber & Bhatt 2007). That entire class of individuals is already in the funnel and thus a potential threat. In operational terms, the NYPD's analysis means that almost the whole young, male Muslim population of urban areas in the US constitutes a threat because they all are in the pre-radicalization stage (Silber & Bhatt 2007).

The report provides five foreign cases of alleged terrorism drawn from incidents in Europe, Canada, Australia and the United States. By aggregating the case studies, the report claims to identify 'typical signatures' associated with each of the four phases. The typical signatures of the preradicalization phase, for example, are '[b]ecoming alienated from one's former life'; '[g]iving up cigarettes, drinking, gambling and urban hip-hop gangster clothes'; '[w]earing traditional Islamic clothing, growing a beard'; and '[b]ecoming involved in social activism and community issues' (Silber & Bhatt 2007). (A subsequent version of the report contained a response to criticism by civil liberties advocates, stating that 'a greater degree of religiosity . . . cannot be used as a signature.') The main text of the report, however, remains unchanged. Signatures of the 'jihadization' phase, in turn, include the undertaking of 'Outward Bound-type activities' and, in one striking passage, the ownership of 'wilted plants', which may be a sign that 'noxious explosives' are being prepared in the location (Silber & Bhatt 2007). The end of the four phases is an acceptance of an 'individual duty to participate in *jihad*' that precedes any 'operational planning for *jihad* or a terrorist attack' (Silber & Bhatt 2007). In the wake of the NYPD's report, the Pennsylvania Municipal Police Officers' Education and Training Commission issued a training manual entitled *Radical Islam: A Law Enforcement Primer*, which merits attention as an elaboration of state-level operational approaches to counterterrorism. The authors did not, however, include an explicit analysis of the process of radicalization with anything like the NYPD report's level of detail. The manual's first section, 'Typologies and Misconceptions', instead contains a disordered sequence of terms, definitions and notes on early Muslim history. The discussion moves indiscriminately, and confusingly, between historical and theological claims. It drifts from doctrinal issues such as a definition of the Sunnah to complex theological notions, such as the abrogation of early verses of the Qur'an by later ones (Kaiser, undated). The manual's second section is entitled 'Radical Islam' and begins with a one-page summary of Islamic theology from the thirteenth-century Ibn Taymiyyah to the twentieth-century Sayyed Qutb (Kaiser, undated). This section gives the impression that a centuries-long sweep of Islamic intellectual and theological development can be distilled down to a single thread: the endorsement of violence for political ends. The third and final section continues the same theme, identifying 'modern radical groups' including Al-Qaeda, Hamas, Islamic Jihad, and Hezbollah, that share 'five pillars of radical ideology' despite the fact that one (Hezbollah) emerges from Shia Islam, which is quite separate from and often antagonistic to the Sunni tradition from which the others emerge (Kaiser, undated). While glossing over elemental differences, *The Primer's* mosaic of disparate facts communicates the impression that the problem of violent terrorism is not linked to a small fraction of Muslims, but rather adheres in the structure and dictates of the faith tradition itself (Huq 2010).

Whereas state models of radicalization have been powerfully informed by a view about the underlying threat level and a normative vision of religious tradition, the US federal response has been fragmented, hesitant, incomplete. No federal agency has published a formal analysis of radicalization. Congress has passed no law directly relating to the matter but the Federal Bureau of Investigation (FBI) and the Department of Homeland Security (DHS) have separately suggested definitions in the course of congressional testimony. In addition, one Senate committee has generated reports that, though heavily dependent on the NYPD's efforts, strive to make a distinctive contribution. In general, federal responses have demonstrated a more tempered and careful position on religious identity. DHS has also taken positions on the mechanisms of radicalization. Addressing Islamic radicalization, DHS Chief Intelligence Officer Charles Allen distinguished 'radicalization from terrorism by emphasizing the difference between related social patterns that may all lead to terrorism' (Chertoff 2007). In the same testimony, Allen cautioned that there are diverse 'pathways' to radicalization, rather than a 'one-way street' (Chertoff 2007). Ideology, including religious ideology, still plays a central role in the DHS account. A key part of the radicalization path, Secretary Chertoff explained, is that 'people have to be persuaded' and 'presented with a comprehensive world narrative' (HSGAC 2007a). In that process of persuasion, Allen identified 'a variety of human and institutional catalysts, such as formal and informal religious institutions' and '[c]harismatic leaders', and risk factors such as '[i]nsular communities with little exposure to moderating influences' and the 'deterioration of familial, social and societal ties' that may precipitate radicalization (Chertoff 2007). In the hearing, Allen indicated prisons and 'university group[s]' as radicalizing hubs (Chertoff 2007). It seems the DHS' understanding of radicalization is in transition. Chertoff mentioned that although DHS was taking 'a comprehensive approach' to the issue, it was still working with the academic and scientific communities in '[d]eveloping a better understanding of the radicalization phenomenon' through cooperation with British counterparts (Chertoff 2007).

In late 2008, DHS issued a request for participation, asking private 'experts . . . to participate in a radicalization-research effort' to 'systematically identify key intervention strategies that can help to prevent or counter radicalization in the United States' (Huq 2010). Like DHS, the National Counter Terrorism Center publicly articulated a multifactor model of radicalization attuned to complex social and psychological nuances. The Congress, too, has started to take a position in the radicalization debate. Since September 2006, the US Senate Committee on Homeland

Security and Governmental Affairs (HSGAC), led by Senators Susan Collins and Joseph Lieberman, has held hearings about the problem of 'domestic radicalization'. The first hearing focused on 'prison radicalization' (HSGAC 2008). In a May 2008 committee report, the HSGAC adopted the NYPD's *Radicalization in the West* analysis (HSGAC 2008). Senator Lieberman lauded the NYPD's analysis as a 'breakthrough' that 'set the standard' for law enforcement (HSGAC 2007b). The HSGAC's contribution to radicalization literature focused on the Internet. In a May 2008 report, the HSGAC concluded that the Internet 'play[s] a critical role throughout the radicalization process'. In its view, the Internet is a bridge by which radicalizing influences enter the US. It is 'the most significant factor in the radicalization process today' (HSGAC 2008). The Internet, on this account, is a way for individuals to find and explore propaganda, to become indoctrinated in the cause, and to connect 'with the global Islamist terrorist movement' (HSGAC 2008). According to the HSGAC, the Internet presents new problems for law enforcement because 'self-generated violent Islamist extremists who are radicalized online' are unlikely to come to law enforcement's attention through real-world activities. The report gives two examples of the Internet's radicalizing potential. One involves two students of the Georgia Institute of Technology who made contact with a Toronto-based group via the Internet; the other is the case of Derrick Shareef, alleged to have been planning an explosives attack on an Illinois mall. In both cases, it is unclear whether the Internet played a unique role that could not have been played by telephone communications (Huq 2010).

The UK Home Office has developed the second important model. The British model on radicalization emerged from a four-dimensional counterterrorism strategy called 'CONTEST'. The 'preventing terrorism' or 'Prevent' strand of CONTEST, implicates the radicalization problem although it is not clear what model of radicalization the British government used up to 2006, when the CONTEST strategy was first released to the public. In early 2005, the Joint Terrorism Analysis Centre (JTAC), part of the British security services, had developed a 'three-tier model . . . to describe the varying degree of connection between targets and the Al-Qaeda leadership', with the tiers corresponding to direct links, loose affiliations, and ideological affinities (ISC 2005). This three-tier model is not elaborated in any public document, and appears to have been abandoned. There is some evidence that the 7 July 2005 London bombings prompted a significant shift in British governmental understanding. According to testimony from the head of specialist operations at the Metropolitan Police Service to Parliament's Intelligence and Security Committee, the security services had until 2005 been 'working off a script which actually has been completely discounted from what we know as reality'.[1] Whatever the old script was, it was formally superseded by 2006. The first prong of the Contest strategy, Prevent, is now dedicated to 'preventing terrorism by tackling the radicalization of individuals' (PM & SSHD 2007). Prevent, in turn is made up of three major strands: ameliorating institutional weaknesses and gaps, hindering extremists from spreading their messages, and winning the hearts and minds of UK's civil society, particularly Britain's marginalized population.

The first official analysis of radicalization by the British government was introduced in 2006 in *Countering International Terrorism: The United Kingdom's Strategy* (PM & SSHD 2007). Publication of this strategy paper came only two months after the Parliamentary Intelligence and Security Committee warned that 'across the whole of the counter-terrorism community the development of the home-grown threat and the radicalism of

[1] Reviewing British counterterrorism strategy in 2004, lawyer John Upton identified Professor Magnus Ranstorp of the Centre for the Study of Terrorism at the University of St. Andrews as a formative influence on UK governmental thinking about 'radicalization'. Ranstorp had a 'four-stage process by which al-Qaida's jihadists are formed. First, a recruit undergoes spiritual preparation; then he is provided with basic military and survival skills. Following this it is his duty to place himself at the fault-lines between Islam and the West; the armed struggle comes last'; also see Upton (2004). This appears to be a different four-stage process from the one offered by the NYPD. What one makes of the proliferation of overlapping models—evidence of intellectual ferment or symptoms of pathological uncertainty—is unclear.

British citizens were not fully understood or applied to strategic thinking' (ISC 2005). The 2006 paper can be read as a response to that challenge. According to *Countering International Terrorism*, radicalization is the first of two steps that may lead to violence. First, an individual alienated from larger society adopts extreme views, thereby becoming radicalized (PM & SSDH 2007). Second, a 'tiny minority' of these radicalized individuals become terrorists 'by financing, lending facilities to, or encouraging active terrorists, or by actively participating in terrorist attacks'. The paper cautions that '[t]he processes whereby certain experiences and events in a person's life cause them to become radicalized, to the extent of turning to violence to resolve perceived grievances, are critical to understanding how terrorist groups recruit new members and sustain support for their activities' (PM & SSHD 2007). But the report adds that this is neither a predictable nor a mechanical process: 'There is a range of potential factors in radicalization and no single factor predominates. It is likely that the catalyst for any given individual becoming a terrorist will be a combination of different factors particular to that person' including a 'sense of grievance and injustice', 'a sense of personal alienation or community disadvantage', and 'exposure to radical ideas' (PM & SSHD 2007).

The 2008 Prevent strategy paper identified five interacting elements with causal links to 'violent extremism': (1) 'an ideology which justifies terrorism by manipulating theology as well as history and politics'; (2) 'radicalizers and their networks'; (3) vulnerable individuals; (4) the lack of community capacity to resist radicalization; and (5) perceived and actual grievances against nation and government (PM & SSHD 2007). Psychological and domestic factors have thus been incorporated with international dynamics. In an appendix, the strategy paper provides an inventory of factors influencing radicalization. This appendix treats radicalization as an individual process, in which factors such as a personal crisis, underemployment, social exclusion, and links to criminality as important elements (PM & SSHD 2007). The appendix further tethers radicalization to the presence of radicalizing 'propagandists, ideologues, or terrorists' and 'extremist material' (PM & SSHD 2007). The implicit account of radicalization here is closer to the American socio-psychological model of personal crisis and resolution through conversion than to *Countering International Terrorism's* effort to take political motivations seriously (Huq 2010). Indeed, political motives are largely absent. Subsequent analyses of radicalization published under the Prevent umbrella also focus on immediate social circumstances rather than national or international political grievances.

The Prevent strategy leaves several key questions unanswered. For example, like the *Countering International Terrorism* paper, it does not adopt a coherent definition of 'radical' that distinguishes between political and religious connections for measuring extremism. Nor does it provide a framework to understand the underlying differences between 'radical' and 'moderate'. But the strategy paper does not explain how 'correct' representations of Islam are to be identified. Second, the Prevent strategy paper introduces a new term, 'violent extremism', to refer to what was earlier called 'radicalism' without explaining the new term. The term 'violent extremism' is discussed at more length in a Department for Education and Skills report on radicalization on college campuses (DES 2006). This report defines '[u]nacceptable extremism' as a spectrum of conduct 'from incitement of social, racial or religious hatred, to advocating the use of violence to achieve fundamental change to the constitutional structure of the United Kingdom, to carrying out terrorist acts'. It cautions that individuals 'can and do' hold extreme views but 'authorities are concerned [only] with any form of extremism that espouses, promotes or leads to violence—'violent extremism' (DES 2006).

The third major model has been designed by the Council of the European Union (CEU). The EU Strategy for Combating Radicalization and Recruitment to Terrorism states that 'radicalization and recruitment to terrorism are not confined to one belief system or political persuasion. Europe has experienced different types of terrorism in its history. But the terrorism perpetrated by Al-Qaeda and extremists inspired by Al-Qaeda has become the main terrorist threat to the EU. While other types of terrorism continue to pose a serious threat to EU citizens, its response to radicalization and recruitment focuses on this type of terrorism' (CEU 2005a). The European Union Counter-Terrorism Strategy, published in 2005, introduces four main strands of EU action; prevent, protect, pursue, respond (CEU 2005b). This document outlines the most prioritized counterterrorism measures of the EU and provides the basis for all other policy documents concerning counterterrorism and radicalization. In line with these strands, in 2005, the EU came forth with the *European Union Strategy for Combating Radicalization and Recruitment to Terrorism*. This document outlined policy measures designed specifically to counter the threat of radicalization and recruitment. In 2007, the EU introduced its *Strategy for Combating Radicalization and Recruitment Implementation Report*, outlining how the designed interventions should be implemented by independent member states. The strategies are further supplemented by (4) the EU Counter-Terrorism Action Plan from 2007, an annual update to account for the progress and status of the implementation of specified measures.

Countering radicalization and recruitment falls under the prevent strand, whose main goal is to 'prevent people from turning to terrorism by tackling the factors or root causes which can lead to radicalization and recruitment, in Europe and internationally' (CEU 2005a). It is paramount to 'prevent people from turning to terrorism and to stop the next generation of terrorists from emerging' (CEU 2005a). Therefore, the EU is committed to 'identify and counter the methods, propaganda and conditions through which people are drawn into terrorism', and to spot and disrupt radical behaviour. Being aware that globalization and the EU's openness enable radical groups to act on their ideas, the EC considers the existence of propagation of extremist world views to be the core issue. For example, propaganda that distorts conflicts around the world as supposed proof of a clash between the West and Islam. To address these issues, the EC aims to ensure that 'voices of mainstream opinion prevail over those of extremism by engaging with civil society and faiths groups that reject the ideas put forward by terrorists and extremists that incite violence' (CEU 2005a). Further, the EU pays special attention to the way its own message comes across, to change the perception of national and European policies and ensure that its own policies do not exacerbate division (EC 2008).

The EU policy responses focus on certain elements in society that may create an environment for radicalization. To counter this and to ensure the long-term integration of minority groups, the EU promotes vigorously good governance, human rights, democracy as well as education and economic prosperity, and engages in conflict resolution. It also aims to 'target inequalities and discrimination where they exist and promote inter-cultural dialogue and long-term integration where appropriate' (CEU 2005a). Finally, the EU perceives radicalization and recruitment as an international phenomenon, where much of the terrorist threat has roots in parts of the world beyond the EU. Therefore, the EU finds cooperation with and the provision of assistance to priority third countries—including in North Africa, the Middle East, South and South-East Asia—to be vital. According to the EU, an 'international dialogue and alliance between cultures faiths and civilizations', is crucial 'to address the motivational and structural factors underpinning radicalization (CEU 2005a). *The Strategy for Combating Radicalization and Recruitment to Terrorism* builds forth on the EU Counter-Terrorism Strategy. The combating recruitment strategy has been particularly designed to curb the threat of violent radicalization, by preventing 'individuals from turning to violence, while halting the emergence of the next generation of terrorists' (CEU 2005a). The EC starts out with a few premises. First, although the EU has witnessed several types of terrorism in its history, this strategy is aimed at terrorism perpetrated by Al-Qaeda and the groups it inspires, as this kind of terrorism currently poses the main threat to the EU. Further, the EU emphasizes that the 'vast majority of Europeans, irrespective of belief, do not accept extremist ideology, and that among the small number that do, only a few turn to terrorism' (CEU 2005a). Regarding Muslim communities in Europe, the EU stresses that 'the overwhelming majority of people espouse the values of peace and tolerance'

(CEU 2005a). Lastly, though the strategy includes practical steps to address radicalization and recruitment, the EU admits it is 'continuing to increase its understanding of the issues' to develop an appropriate response (CEU 2005a).

In identifying and countering 'the ways, propaganda and conditions through which people are drawn into terrorism and consider it a legitimate course of action', the EU resolves to attain three main goals (EC 2008). First, it aims to 'disrupt the activities of the networks and individuals who draw people into terrorism' (EC 2008). The main premise is that individuals must take practical steps to engage with terrorism. Therefore, the EU 'works' to spot suspicious behaviour, for instance by monitoring the Internet and travel to conflict zones. It aims to disrupt this behaviour, by 'limiting the activities of those playing a role in radicalization', including in prisons, places of religious training and worship, and the Internet (EC 2008). The EU also strives to prevent individuals from gaining access to terrorist training, for instance by monitoring travel to conflict zones. Finally, the EU works towards a 'right legal framework to prevent individuals from inciting and legitimizing violence' (CEU 2005a).

The second aim of the strategy is to ensure that 'voices of mainstream opinion prevail over those of extremism' (CEU 2005a). As stated earlier, the EU considers extremist propaganda to be crucial, especially propaganda which depicts international conflicts as proof of the clash between the West and Islam. The EC is committed to counter propagation that 'claims to give individuals both an explanation for grievances and an outlet for their anger' (CEU 2005a). To do so, the EU aims to empower moderate Islamic voices, for instance through cooperation with Muslim organizations and faith groups and the encouragement of the emergence of European *imams*. Further, the EU aims to 'coordinate and enhance our efforts to change the perceptions of European and Western policies particularly among Muslim communities, and to correct unfair or inaccurate perceptions of Islam and Muslims' (CEU 2005a). The EC seeks to avoid the linkage between Islam and terrorism at all times, for instance by developing a non-emotive lexicon for discussing sensitive issues.

Third, the EU aims to 'promote yet more vigorously security, justice, democracy and opportunity for all' (CEU 2005a). This goal, earlier mentioned in the Counter-Terrorism Strategy, is designed to respond to conditions in society that might create an environment for radicalism. According to the EU, these conditions include a lack of political and economic prospects, unresolved international and domestic strife, and inadequate and inappropriate education or cultural opportunities for young people, among others. The EC adds that these conditions may be particularly present in immigrant communities. To address these issues, the EU aims to target 'inequalities and discrimination where they exist and promote inter-cultural dialogue, debate and, where appropriate, long-term integration' internally (CEU 2005a). Outside Europe, the EU works to 'promote good governance, human rights, democracy, as well as education and economic prosperity', as well as conflict resolution (CEU 2005a).

However, what are missing here are the psychological dynamics and the 'choices' that presumably influence an individual to undertake radical courses. The choices and decisions people make are to a large extent based on their personal experiences. Therefore, at the individual level, experiences influence how people respond to their social and external environment. It seems that major life events, such as a traumatizing and abusive childhood, can lead to radicalization. Although the EU does highlight the central role individual motives play in radicalization processes, personal backgrounds and experiences as prominent causes are not discussed in either of the strategies concerning radicalization. Individuals radicalize for different reasons, of which some are more conscious than others. Examples of intentions why people join a radical group include adventurous reasons, obtaining a specific identity, or ideological motivations. Therefore, the question arises whether radicalism is a product of rational choice. The strategy argues that radicalization is usually a gradual process, and thus a state of mind, rather than a tool that is employed to achieve a goal.

In its strategies, the EU indicates that an individual must take practical steps to become involved in terrorism, and that 'the decision to become involved in terrorism is an individual one'

(CEU 2005b). However, despite the emphasis that is laid on the role of the individual in radicalization and terrorism, no mention is made of rational choice being a reason for radicalism in the strategies. Of course, this factor is linked to the types of causes at the external level—political, economic, cultural causes. However, like the UK strategy, the EU document registers a list of issues that identifies a range of conditions in society, which may create an environment in which people can more easily be radicalized. Such factors do not necessarily lead to radicalization, but may make the radical message more appealing both to those who suffer them and those who identify with their suffering. According to the EU model, these conditions may include poor or autocratic governance; states moving from autocratic control via inadequate reform to partial democracy; rapid but unmanaged modernization; and lack of political and economic prospects, unresolved international and domestic strife; and inadequate and inappropriate education or cultural opportunities for young people. Within the EU, most of these factors are not present, but within individual segments of the population, they may apply and there may also be issues of identity in immigrant communities (CEU 2005a).

IMPLICATIONS OF THE MODELS

The models we have discussed present a blatant consistency in the radicalization process, which is neither predictable nor mechanical: 'There are a range of potential factors in radicalization and no single factor predominates. It is likely that the catalyst for any given individual becoming a terrorist will be a combination of different factors particular to that person' including a 'sense of grievance and injustice', 'a sense of personal alienation or community disadvantage', and the 'exposure to radical ideas' (PM & SSDH 2007). That is to say that radicalization is not a unified and linear concept (Huq 2010). The cases of terrorism, as discussed in Chapter Three, denote that radicalization occurs using two steps, where in the first step an individual alienated from larger society adopts extreme views, thereby becoming radicalized. Second, an 'insignificant minority in terms of demographic size' of these radicalized individuals become terrorists 'by financing, lending facilities to, or encouraging active terrorists, or by actively participating in terrorist attacks' (Huq 2010). It also shows that radicalization is a process whereby individual's experiences and encounter with various incidents in life may cause them to become radicalized.

Comparison between the trends in radicalization discourse and the models studied suggests that there are no predictable paths to violence. However, it signifies several factors including political, social, and religious elements such as: globalization and its discontents (Stiglitz 2002), personal alienation, or economic or social disadvantage; and exposure to radical ideas or an inspiring figure already committed to extremism (PM & SSDH 2007). These factors emphasize on faith and personal, psychological dynamics, as well as endorse deep political roots. However, what is problematic here is that none of these factors seem sufficient, or necessary, in the path towards terrorism.[2] The challenge to these models lies in their inadequacies in understanding that most of the South Asians share similar backgrounds and experiences but only few of them become radicalized. Therefore, radicalization in South Asia, in particular, cannot be defined solely in terms of 'violence'.

[2] For an overview of the empirical literature, see Kruglanski and Fishman (2006). Their comparative research found no specific psychological behaviours that could be considered as common elements among the terrorists.

CHAPTER FIVE

Why Conventional Wisdom on Radicalization Fails

SIMPLIFICATION AND THE BINARY VIEWS

Conventional wisdom and models on radicalization appear to fail at various levels of analysis. Radicalization models, as illustrated in the earlier part of this study, show that there is little evidence to endorse that cultural or social differences among Muslims are causing violent radicalization. Both the South Asian and Western counterterrorism and security strategists make certain assumptions about the causes of radicalization. These assumptions signify a tension between simplification of the causes and historical justifications of 'hatred'. A simplistic binary view of the South Asian Muslims or immigrant Muslims to the West as either 'violent' or 'moderate' alienates the majority of Muslims who view Islam as a faith, not a political ideology, and who identify themselves primarily as citizens of their respective countries where they live, not as members of a transnational political community. The response to radicalization gets further complicated due to the awkward task of the Western governments to promote Western values in the Eastern circles. So far, policy-makers, both in South Asia and in the West, to a large extent, formulate their policy responses on the models of radicalization mentioned in the earlier chapter. However, these models not only suffer from methodological and substantive shortcomings but also produce negatively informed policies. This study also shows how it would be far too simplistic to say that radicalization is caused by the absence of democracy.

These observations suggest that, at the very least, simplification and stereotyping of any 'identity' cannot be associated with radicalization. It is clear even from the brief examination of the public policies in the US, the UK, the EU and South Asian states that approaches to counterterrorism and/or counter-radicalization that assume the existence of simple 'root causes' or 'pathways' are not only naïve but may actually be counterproductive. In other words, it is the perception rather than the objective situation that is relevant in the emergence of radicalization. To gain a further insight into the relationship between direct and indirect causes of radicalization, it is essential to map the complex interactions between the driving factors at different levels and dimensions (Veldhuis & Staun 2009). An important lesson learned from the history of right- and left-wing radicalization in South Asia and Europe is that identity is gaining increasing prominence. The literatures in Chapters Two and Three in this study indicate that it is important to understand the complex and diverse reasons for the foregrounding of religion as a maker of identity by different extremist groups. One reason is that there is something intrinsic to religion that leads to greater demands for public accommodation. The second reason sees mobilization as a reaction to discrimination and socio-economic deprivation. Muslim mobilization as a response to the public devaluation and disparagement of Muslims and Islam has led to increased in-group solidarity. Thus, extremism as a decisive factor, at times emerges as a reaction against the state, combined with dramatic increase in ethnic tension.

Further, social factors appear to intervene at every level of analysis beginning from individuals to social groups to state. For example, the degree to which people identify with a relevant social group determines the extent to which they are affected by political, economic and cultural circumstances. It means that the 'perception', along with objective situation, is relevant to understanding the emergence of radicalization. Therefore, radicalization also creates opportunities for those seeking to establish normative distance from the state (Meyer 2004). The state supplies its own counter-narrative by legitimizing certain forms of resistance. As a result, radicalization can be seen, perhaps not without irony, as a path of resistance and individuation through the tailoring of a readymade mould of counter-cultural resistance. It remains to be seen how these openings and resources are leveraged in the creation of new political and religious identities over the future course of South Asian history. More research is also required to scrutinize the differences between radicalization processes that find their roots in ideological concerns about the state, and radicalization processes that are products of social dynamics.

CONCLUSION

The views and theoretical contexts assembled here address problems in understanding and issues in radicalization in South Asia. From the beginning, care was taken to ensure that all factors dealt with—all of them enormously controversial—would be addressed from a diversity of philosophical and constructivist points of view. Thus, neither 'theoretical perspective' nor 'theoretical solution' could be found in South Asia. This study has identified that the contemporary manifestation of South Asian version of Islam, which involves complex geographies and institutions and its transnational diaspora, problematizes conventional categorization of resistance and political ideologies through frequent cross-fertilization across political and extremist tendencies. This study further suggests that the emerging geography of globalized Islam and statist Hinduism calls into question the extent to which political manifestations of these religions can be analysed with exclusive reference to local circumstances or sources of discontent. Further, the radicalization discourse may influence front-end decisions about what conduct to criminalize, or charging decisions under embryonic statutes, such as the material support to terrorism provisions (Huq 2010). Finally, different understandings of the relation of terrorism to religious or ethnic identity may alter tolerance levels for contextual intolerance within the statist and societal institutions. A major challenge was to maintain throughout the study a commitment to impartial, unfettered, and rigorous scholarly inquiry. Naturally, this does not mean that a reader will find the argument in each part entirely appealing. However, the contents of this study may stimulate closer attention, for policy-makers as well as academic analysts, to the widespread, multifaceted and profoundly important phenomenon of radicalization in South Asia.

Bibliography

Ahmed, I. (2005), 'On the Brink of Precipice: Contemporary Terrorism and the Limits of the State', Keynote paper presented at the Institute of Diploma Engineers, Kakrail, organized by Bangladesh Foundation for Development Research, Dhaka, on 30 November 2005.

Aiyar, Swaminathan S. Anklesaria. (2001), 'Terrorism Is Certainly Not A Muslim Monopoly', *Fact of Arabs*, available online at www.factofarabs.net/ERA.aspx?Id=667&TId=58,lastaccessedon29August 2011.

Akbar, M.J. (1988), *Riot After Riot: Reports on Caste and Communal Violence in India*, New Delhi: Roli Books.

Armstrong, K. (2001), *The Battle for God: A History of Fundamentalism*, New York: Ballantine.

Azad, M.A.K. (1988), *India Wins Freedom*, New Delhi: Orient Longman.

Azra, A. (2005), 'Islam in Southeast Asia: Tolerance and Radicalism', paper presented at Miegunyah Public Lecture, The University of Melbourne, 6 April 2005, available online at www.bgu.edu/sitemedia/_courses/reading/art2-islam.pdf, last accessed on 5 May 2011.

Bearak, B. (2001), 'Death to Blasphemers: Islam's Grip on Pakistan', *New York Times,* 12 May 2001, online edition last accessed on 11 June 2011.

Breen Smyth, M., J. Gunning, R. Jackson, G. Kassimeris, and P. Robinson (2008), 'Critical Terrorism Studies: An Introduction', *Critical Studies On Terrorism*, vol. 1(1), pp. 1–4.

CEU (Council of the European Union) (2005a), *The European Union Strategy for Combating Radicalization and Recruitment to Terrorism*, Brussels: European Commission. available online at http://register.consilium.eu.int/pdf/en/05/st14/st14781-re01.en05.pdf, last accessed on 1 September 2011.

——— (2005b), *The European Union Counter-Terrorism Strategy*, Brussels:

European Commission. available online at http://register.consilium.eu.int/pdf/en/05/st14/st14469-re04.en05.pdf, last accessed on 1 September 2011.

Chandhoke, Neera (2001), *Security in Times of Hindutva?* Hawaii: Asia-Pacific Center for Security Studies.

Chertoff, Michael (2007), 'Testimony Before the Senate Committee on Homeland Security and Government Affairs', 110th Congress, written testimony of Michael Chertoff, Secretary of the Department of Homeland Security, available online at http://hsgac.senate.gov/public/_files/031407Chertoff.pdf, last accessed on 19 September 2011.

Choudhury, T. (2007), *The Role of Muslim Identity Politics in Radicalization (A Study in Progress)*, Department for Communities and Local Government, UK, available online at www.communities.gov.uk/documents/communities/pdf/452628.pdf, last accessed on 27 August 2011.

Cohen, S.P. (2004), *The Idea of Pakistan*, Washington, DC: Brooking Institution Press.

DES (Department for Education and Skills) (2006), *Promoting Good Campus Relations: Working With Staff and Students to Build Community Cohesion and Tackle Violent Extremism in the Name of Islam at Universities and Colleges*, available online at www.dcsf.gov.uk/hegateway/uploads/ExtremismGuidancefinal.pdf, last accessed on 7 June 2011.

Desai, Meghnad (2005), *Development and Nationhood: Essays in the Political Economy of South Asia*, New Delhi: Oxford University Press.

EC (European Commission) (2008), *The EU Counterradicalization Strategy: Evaluating EU Policies Concerning Causes of Radicalization, Workpackage 4, Objective 6,* available online at www.transnationalterrorism.eu/tekst/publications/EU%20Counterradicalization%20Strategy.pdf, last accessed on 1 September 2011.

Engineer, Asghar Ali (1991), *Communal Riots in Post-Independent India*, New Delhi: Orient Longman, p. 278.

GFF (Global Futures Forum) (2006), *Radicalization, Violence and the Power of Networks* [Report of the Autumn 2006 Brussels Workshop], Brussels: GFF.

Ganguly, S. (2000), 'Pakistan's Never-Ending Story', *Foreign Affairs*, vol. 79, no. 2 (March/April 2000), p. 6.

Gurr, T. (1970), *Why Men Rebel*, Princeton, New Jersey: Princeton University Press.

Haqqani, H. (2005a), 'The Ideologies of South Asian Jihadi Groups', *Current Trends in Islamist Ideologies,* vol. 1, Hudson Institute, Inc.: New York, available online at www.carnegieendowment.org/files/Ideologies.pdf, last accessed on 1 September 2011.

——— (2005b), *Pakistan: Between Mosque and Military*, Washington, DC: Carnegie Endowment for International Peace.

Hashmi, Taj I. (1994), 'Islam in Bangladesh Politics', in Mutalib Hussain, and Taj I. Hashmi (eds), *Islam, Muslims and the Modern State*, London: Macmillan, pp. 110–13.

——— (2004), 'Islamic Resurgence in Bangladesh: Genesis, Dynamics and Implications', in S. Limaye (ed.) (2004), *Religious Radicalism and Security in South Asia*, available online at www.apcss.org/wp-content/uploads/2010/PDFs/Edited%20Volumes/Religious Radicalism//ReligiousRadicalismandSecurityinSouth Asia.pdf, last accessed on 14 February 2012.

HSGAC (Homeland Security and Governmental Affairs Committee) (2007a), 'Transcript of 14 March 2007, US Senate Homeland Security and Governmental Affairs Committee Hearing on Islamist Radicalization at 2 (Sen. Joseph I. Lieberman)', available online at http://hsgac.senate.gov/public/index.cfm?FuseAction=Hearings.Hearing&Hearing_ID=2fb6902f-72e9-45a6-b5b2-15389ed18ec3, last accessed on 19 September 2011.

——— (2007b), 'Sen. Lieberman Applauds Pioneering Report on Homegrown Islamic Radicalism, Senate Committee on Homeland Security and Governmental Affairs, 15 August 2007', available online at http://hsgac.senate.gov/public/index.cfm?FuseAction=Press.MajorityNews&ContentRecord_id=350f95d1-d9bf-446e-b6a3-c3d13df07a56&Region_id=&Issue_id, last accessed on 19 September 2011.

——— (2008), 'Violent Islamist Extremism, The Internet, and the Homegrown Terrorist Threat: Majority & Minority Staff Report: Hearing Before the Senate Committee on Homeland Security and Governmental Affairs'. 110th Congress 4 (2008), available online at http://hsgac.senate.gov/public/_files/IslamistReport.pdf, last accessed on 19 September 2011.

——— (2006), 'Prison Radicalization: are Terrorist Cells Forming in U.S. Prison Blocks?: Hearing Before the Senate Committee on Homeland Security and Governmental Affairs', available online at http://hsgac.senate.gov/public/index.cfm?FuseAction=Hearings.Hearing&Hearing_ID=b602edb5-1faa-4011-b12c-c312678d1b71, last accessed on 19 September 2011.

Huq, A. (2010), 'Modeling Terrorist Radicalization', *Public Law and Legal Theory Working Paper*, No. 301, available online at www.law.uchicago.edu/academics/publiclaw/index.html, last accessed on 20 September 2011

ISC (Intelligence and Security Committee) (2005). 'Report into the London Terrorist Attack on 7 July 2005', available online at www.cabinetoffice.gov.uk/media/cabinetoffice/corp/assets/publications/reports/intelligence/isc_7july_report.pdf revised 2006-2007, last accessed on 7 June 2011.

Kamal, Ahmed (1989), 'A Land of Eternal Eid: Independence, People and Politics in East Bengal', *Dhaka University Studies*, 46, June 1989, p. 81.

Khan, S.E. (2010), Keynote and inaugural paper on 'Understanding the Threats from the Islamist Extremists in Bangladesh', Conference on 'India–Bangladesh Dialogue on Security', 19–20 March 2010, New Delhi: Observer Research Foundation.

——— (2012), 'US Foreign Policy toward Bangladesh: Implications of the Rise of Islamist Terrorism', in B.M. Rajaee and M.J. Miller (eds) (2012), *National Security under the Obama Administration*, New York: Palgrave Macmillan.

Kruglanski, A.W. and S. Fishman (2006), 'The Psychology of Terrorism: Syndrome vs Tool Perspective', *Terrorism and Political Violence*, vol. 18, pp. 193–215, available online at www.un.org/depts/dhl/resources/terrorism/toc/toc5.pdf, last accessed on 7 June 2011

Kumar, R. (2004), 'Religious Radicalism and Minorities in South Asia', Chapter 18, pp. 437–446, in S. Limaye (ed.) (2004), *Religious Radicalism and Security in South Asia*, available online at www.apcss.org/wp-content/uploads/2010/PDFs/Edited%20Volumes/ReligiousRadicalism//ReligiousRadicalismandSecurityinSouthAsia.pdf, last accessed on 15 October 2011.

Kurth, J. (2002), 'Confronting the Unipolar Moment: The American Empire and Islamic Terrorism', *Current History*, p. 404.

Luce, E. (2006), *In Spite of the Gods: The Strange Rise of Modern India*, London: Abacus.

Mandel, D.R. (in press). 'Radicalization: What Does it Mean?', in T. Pick and A. Speckhard (eds), *Indigenous Terrorism: Understanding and Addressing the Root Causes of Radicalization Among Groups with an Immigrant Heritage in Europe*, Amsterdam: IOS Press, available online at http://individual.utoronto.ca/mandel/Mandel-radicalization.pdf

Meyer, D.S. (2004), 'Protest and Political Opportunities', *Annual Review of Sociology*, vol. 30, pp. 125–45.

NATOSA (North Atlantic Treaty Organization Standardization Agency) (2007), *Allied Administrative Publication*, no. 6 (AAP-6), Brussels: NATOSA, available online at www.fas.org/irp/doddir/other/nato2008.pdf, last accessed on 27 August 2011.

Nehru, J. (1946), *The Discovery of India*, New York: Doubleday.

Neumann, P.R. (2008), 'Introduction', in P.R. Neumann, J. Stoil and D. Esfandiary (eds), *Perspectives on Radicalization and Political Violence: Papers from The First International Conference on Radicalization and Political Violence*, London: International Centre for the Study of Radicalization and Political Violence, pp. 2–7.

Oneindia News (2010), *Hindu Extremists 'Bigger Threat' to India than Muslim Militants: Rahul Gandhi to US*. Friday, 17 December 2010, available online at http://news.oneindia.in/2010/12/17/hinduextremists-bigger-threat-to-india-than-muslimmilita.html, last accessed on 27 August 2011.

Pantucci, R. (2008). 'Britain's Prison Dilemma: Issues and Concerns in Islamic Radicalization', *Terrorism Monitor,* vol. 6(6), pp. 6–8, Washington, DC: The Jamestown Foundation.

Kaiser, B. (ed.) (undated), *Radical Islam: A Law Enforcement Primer*, Municipal Police Officers' Education & Training Commission, Pennsylvania State Police.

Pape, R.A. (2006). 'Suicide Terrorism and Democracy: What We've Learned since 9/11', *Policy Analysis*, Issue No. 582, Cato Institute, available online at http://www.cato.org/pubs/pas/pa582.pdf, last accessed on 15 October 2011.

PM & SSDH (Prime Minister and Secretary of State for the Department of Home) (2007). Countering International Terrorism: United Kingdom's Strategy, 2006–07, Cm. 6888, at 1–4. Available at http://www.iwar.org.uk/homesec/resources/uk-threat-level/uk-counterterrorism-strategy.pdf Accessed on 7 December 2011.

Sageman, M. (2007), *Radicalization of Global Islamist Terrorists*, Testimony presented to US Senate Committee on Homeland Security and Governmental Affairs, available online at www.globalfuturesforum.org/ReadingDetail.php?rid=520, last accessed on 11 May 2011.

Sahai, S. (1997), *India: Twilight at Midday*, Gyan: Delhi.

Said, E. (1979), *Orientalism*, Vintage: Massachusetts, p. 23 (for the purpose of this study, adopting the concept of Western texts about the 'Orient').

Sharma, H.C. (1996), 'Chapter III: Communalism in Uttar Pradesh in the 1980s', available online at http://dspace.vidyanidhi.org.in:8080/dspace/bitstream/2009/5758/4/JMI-1996-001-3.pdf, last accessed on 15 October 2011.

Silber, M.D. and A. Bhatt (2007), 'Radicalization in the West: The Homegrown Threat', New York: New York Police Department. available online at www.nypdshield.org/public/SiteFiles/documents/NYPD_Report-Radicalization_in_the_West.pdf, last accessed on 1 September 2011.

Sood, V. (2011), 'Radical Islam in South Asia and Implications for the Region', Chapter 3, pp. 44–77, in V. Sood and S. Kurginyan (2011), *Radical Islam: Perspectives from India and Russia*, New Delhi: Macmillan.

Sood, V. and S. Kurginyan (2011), *Radical Islam: Perspectives from India and Russia*, London: Macmillan.

Stiglitz, J. (2002), *Globalization and Its Discontents*, London: Norton.

Taylor, D. (ed.) (2010), *Islam in South Asia,* New Delhi: Routledge.

Upton, J. (2004). *In the Streets of Londonistan,* London: Reverend Books.

Veldhuis, T. and J. Staun (2009), *Islamist Radicalization: A Root Cause Model*, The Hague: Netherlands Institute of International Relations Clingendael, available online at www.diis.dk/graphics/_IO_indsatsomraader/Religion_og_social_konflikt_og_Mellemosten/Islamist%20Radicalization.Veldhuis%20and%20Staun.pdf, last accessed on 1 October 2011.

Victoroff, J. (2005), 'The Mind of the Terrorist: A Review and Critique of Psychological Approaches', *Journal of Conflict Resolution*, vol. 49, no. 1, pp. 3–42, available online at www.psci.unt.edu/jbooks/terrorbib_files/psychology%20of%20terrorism/victoroff-the%20mind%20of%20the%20terrorist.pdf, last accessed on 1 September 2011.

Wiktorowicz, Q. (2005). *Radical Islam Rising: Muslim Extremism in the West*, California: Rowman & Littlefield.

Wirsing, R. (2004), 'Introduction: Religion, Radicalism, and Security in South Asia', Chapter 1, pp. 1–16, in S. Limaye (ed.) (2004), *Religious Radicalism and Security in South Asia*, available online at w www.apcss.org/wp-content/uploads/2010/PDFs/Edited%20Volumes/ReligiousRadicalism//ReligiousRadicalismandSecurityinSouthAsia.pdf, last accessed on 15 October 2011.

RCSS PUBLICATIONS

- *Defence, Technology and Cooperative Security in South Asia: Report on the Proceedings of the Tenth Summer Workshop* (RCSS, 2004)
- *Environment Development and Human Security: Perspectives from South Asia* (2003)
- *Terrorism in South Asia: Impact on Development and Democratic Process* (SIPRA, 2003)
- *South Asia and the War on Terrorism* (India Research Press, 2003)
- *Shaping the Future—A South Asian Civil Society Dialogue* (RCSS, July 2002)
- *Small Arms and Human Insecurity* (RCSS, July 2002)
- *SAARC in the Twenty-First Century: Towards a Cooperative Future* (July 2002)
- *Memories of a Genocidal Partition: The Haunting Tale of Victims, Witnesses and Perpetrators* (RCSS, July 2002)
- *South Asian Security Futures: A Dialogue of Director's Regional Strategic Studies Institutes* (March 2002)
- *Globalization and Non-Traditional Security in South Asia* (September 2001)
- *The Simla Agreement. i972: Its Wasted Promise* (Manohar, 2001)
- *Ending the Displacement Cycle: Finding Durable Solutions through Return and Resettlement* (RCSS, 2011)
- *Documents on Sri Lanka's Foreign Policy 1947-1965* (RCSS, 2005)
- *Terrorism in South Asia: Impact on Development and Democratic Process* (RCSS & Konrad Adenauer Foundation, 2003)
- *Environment, Development and Human Security: Perspectives from South Asia* (University Press of America, 2003)

RCSS Policy Studies

50 Extremism in Pakistan and India: The Case of Jamaat-e-Islami and Shiv Sena (RCSS, 2010)
49 Democracy as a Conflict Resolution Model for Terrorism: A Case Study of India and Pakistan (RCSS, 2010)
48 Understanding Suicide Terrorism and Bangladesh and Sri Lanka (RCSS, 2010)
47 India's Security Dilemma vis-à-vis China: A Case of Optimum or Sub-Optimum Restraint? (RCSS, 2009)
46 Beyond the Security Impasse: State, Development and People (RCSS, 2008)
45 Conflict Transformation from Ethnic Movement to Terrorist Movement: Case Studies of Tamils in Sri Lanka and Mohajirs in Pakistan (RCSS, 2008)
44 Indo- US Nuclear Cooperation: Altering Strategic Positioning & Shifting Balance of Power in South Asia (RCSS, 2008)
43 Peace Building in Afghanistan: Revisiting the Global War on Terrorism (RCSS, 2008)
42 Getting to Rapprochement over Kashmir: Is Using the 'China Model' a Viable Alternative? (RCSS, 2007)
41 Role of a Third Party in Conflict Resolution: A Case Study of India and Norway in Sri Lanka (RCSS, 2007)
40 International Non-Governmental Organizations in Arms Control and Disarmament Potential and Viability (RCSS, 2007)
39 India- Pakistan Dialogue: Bringing the Society in (RCSS, 2007)
38 The 'People's War' in Nepal (RCSS, 2006)
37 Impact of Partition Refugees in Pakistan: Struggle for Empowerment and State's Response (Manohar, 2006)
36 Maritime Cooperation between India and Sri Lanka (Manohar, 2006)
35 Nuclear Risk Reduction Measures in South Asia: Problems and Prospects (Manohar,2006)
34 Indo-Pak Conflicts: Ripe to Resolve? (Manohar, 2005)
33 Small Arms and the Security Debate in South Asia (Manohar, 2005)